I Believe in The Great Commission

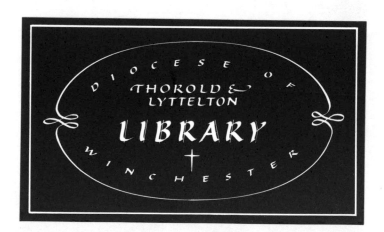

I Believe in The Great Commission

by

MAX WARREN

HODDER AND STOUGHTON
LONDON SYDNEY AUCKLAND TORONTO

To

Rosemary and Greg,

Pat and Roger,

Sheelagh,

and

all on the Frontiers of Obedience

Editor's Preface

I Believe in the Great Commission, writes Max Warren, and he is a bold man to do so. For contemporary Christianity has, for the most part, lost its nerve. We live in an age when everything is relative, nothing absolute; when nothing is black and white, everything different shades of grey. And to maintain that Christianity is true, that Jesus really is the way to God, and that obedience to him inevitably carries with it the imperative to mission, is thoroughly unpopular. It accords ill with contemporary religious agnosticism, apathy, and syncretism. It savours of intolerance and arrogance. Moreover the view that 'They've got their own religions, and are perfectly happy as they are' or that 'In the contemporary economic and international climate, the days of the missionary are over' are frequently advanced, even in church circles. Yes, Dr. Warren is a brave man to write on behalf of so despised and unpopular a subject as mission.

For that very reason this is an important and timely book. Modern Christians need to hear again the challenge of the New Testament to mission. We need to look with realism and a large measure of shame at the course of Christian history, and the way that obedience to the Great Commission has so often been prostituted by subservience to quite other goals, such as economic, political or cultural colonialism. We need to learn from some of the mistakes of the past, but also to recapture the zeal of some past ages of the Church to fulfil the Great Commission. Christian allegiance needs to be rescued from seeming a 'Sundays only' affair: it demands to be brought back firmly into the forefront of our life's aims and our style of living. If the Church is to be recalled effectively to its total mission, it is likely to be at the hands of one who knows the Scriptures, who has himself served in various parts of the world, who has a global vision, and who can combine flexibility of tactics with singleminded strategy. Dr. Max Warren is such a man. Those who have read his autobiography, *Crowded Canvas*, will have perceived something of the breadth of vision, wisdom in counsel, and strength of leadership which made him for so many years such a visionary General Secretary of the Church Missionary Society, and led to his being the sought-after confidant of Christian leaders the world over. His book, written with a cool head, a warm heart, and a ready pen, is a most significant addition to this series which is designed to take a fresh look at controversial areas of the Christian faith. The fact that it is being published along with other volumes in the series, in Britain, the U.S.A. and the Continent will ensure that mission, as a crucial article of Christian faith and obedience, is brought into renewed prominence in many parts of the world where its call badly needs to be heard. The church that lives to itself dies to itself. This book is written from life, to bring life...

Michael Green

Foreword

THE BIBLE HAS a global perspective and a clear end in
view. In the Old Testament this is summed up in the words,
'The glory of the Lord shall be revealed and all mankind
together shall see it' (Isaiah 40:5). The New Testament says the
same thing in its vision of the holy city, symbol of a new
heaven and a new earth, shining with the glory of God, a city
into which the splendour and wealth of the nations shall be
brought (Rev. 21:11, 26).

In the Old Testament the destiny of Israel was to bear
witness to God's purpose. The New Testament is explicit that
the acts of God in history and his supreme revelation in Jesus
Christ are to be made known to all men, with all things in
heaven and earth reconciled in him (Col. 1:20).

No candid student of the Bible can doubt this global
perspective and specific goal. The missionary outreach of the
Church down the centuries has been an attempt to be obedient
to the heavenly vision.

Have we the same confidence? This book has been written
with the conviction that we can have it and should have it. At
the same time I have tried to take seriously the genuine
perplexities in the minds of many Christians who are baffled by
the developments of this century, and who find it hard to see
how obedience to the vision is to be carried out.

The argument begins, as for the Christian it must begin,
with Jesus Christ, his life and death and resurrection. It
continues by way of exploring how the implications of that life,
death and resurrection have gripped the minds of Christians.
Frequent failures to grasp these implications aright are frankly
acknowledged. The Gospel has often been tragically distorted,

but it survives the blunders of its professors. Today, no less than in all our yesterdays, it is proving to be the power of God and the wisdom of God (1 Cor. 1:24).

Our task is to draw on that wisdom and depend on that power for our own responsiblities, and press on to the goal.

Following the directions of the Editor of this Series, I have provided no 'mileage of footnotes'. My indebtedness to countless other minds must therefore be discovered, to a very limited degree, in a short bibliography. The titles of most of the books referred to in the text, as well as those from which quotations are taken, will be found in the bibliography. Again, in obedience to the Editor, I have tried to curb my passion for good quotations. Where, however I touch on controversial matters, some quotations are necessary out of courtesy to those with whom I presume to disagree. I hope my other quotations will illustrate and not confuse.

All the references from the Bible are taken from the New English Bible Translation, unless otherwise noted.

Three personal acknowledgements I must make. The first is to my son-in-law, Roger Hooker, a missionary in North India. With him I have had an almost fortnightly correspondence over the last eleven years. This has kept me in touch with the actual life and work of a foreign missionary. In particular, I have been enabled to live, if only at second-hand, in the creative experience of meeting with men of other Faiths, Hindus, Muslims, Jains, and Buddhists. I have been able to know something of the joy and anguish, the hopes and disappointments of those who seek to interpret Jesus Christ to those of another people for whom he is a stranger. This, for me, has been an immense enrichment. Without it I could not have written this book.

Gratitude also demands another acknowledgement, no less sincerely felt, to Susan Harverson, who has entered so willingly into the work of this book, has raised many a pertinent query, and whose skill in typing has, as every author knows, made all the difference when it came to checking references.

Then I have to thank Michael Green, as the Editor of this Series, for according me the great privilege of writing on this subject. In doing so, he took a higher risk than he knew. He is wholly innocent of any follies I have perpetrated.

Being married to Patience, albeit under another name, calls not for an acknowledgement so much as for an anthology, which, alas, space forbids.

MAX WARREN

Waymarks
East Dean
Nr Eastbourne
January, 1976

Contents

I Believe in The Great Commission

Jesus himself is the Great Commission. He is the Man who is sent. He himself is the Message. In his life and through his teachings and actions, in his dying and his death and by his resurrection, he is the proclamation of his Message. He is its herald. This fundamental affirmation is the theme of the New Testament. As Christians we believe that this theme was foreshadowed in the Old Testament.

If we have here the key to understanding the Bible, then by its faithful witness to this truth, by its worship and its service, the Church lives. Unfaithful, it begins to die.

The authenticity of the Christian Mission in the world today is to be tested by its fidelity to the Word who is Jesus.

These are formidable claims. A spelling out is needed.

Part I — The New Testament spells it out

Part II — The Church in history spells it out

Part III — What spelling it out means today.

PART I

The New Testament Spells It Out

He uttered a triumphant cry: IT IS ACCOMPLISHED! And it was as though he had said: Everything has begun.

Nikos Kazantzakis
The Last Temptation

THE NEW TESTAMENT is a post-Resurrection collection of letters, memoirs, reminiscences, personal testimonies, observations on current events, and, supremely, a number of interpretations of the supreme Event — Jesus of Nazareth, the Christ of God. As such it is invaluable historical evidence of what some people believed about Jesus in the first fifty to seventy years after the Crucifixion. Some of it is the record of eye-witnesses who knew Jesus before the Crucifixion. What these particular sources have to say presents a coherent picture of an historical Person.

We have here an anthology, highly selective (see John 21:25; Luke 1:1-4), on the theme of the centrality of Jesus of Nazareth as being the fullest possible revelation of God, 'found in fashion as a man' (Phil. 2:8 A.V.) that is, 'revealed in human shape'. It is only a selection but a selection to which we can properly attribute the word *inspired*. What inspiration means may not be easy to define. One definition is to be found in Luther's writings where he says 'The words of St. Paul are not dead words; they are living creatures, and have hands and feet.' What is true of St. Paul is true of the whole New Testament, is true of the whole Bible. What follows is an attempt to discover what these 'living creatures' have to tell us.

A 'post-Resurrection collection' is an important phrase whose significance must occupy us further. The entire New Testament is a consistent witness to and an insistence upon the fact that the crucifixion of Jesus, which for most of his devoted friends, perhaps for all of them, was the end, was in truth not the end. Something happened very soon after the dead body of

Jesus had been laid in the tomb. Nobody saw it happen. But a considerable number of people were completely convinced that they did, in the next few weeks, see and talk with this very Jesus whom they knew personally, and who they knew had been crucified, had died and had been buried.

Muslims, and not only Muslims, say that the evidence has been tampered with or, more commonly, that a very vivid spiritual experience has been clothed in the language of historical narrative. 'Why is it considered incredible that God should raise dead men to life?' That was the question which Paul addressed to a Jewish King, Agrippa, an acknowledged expert in all Jewish matters (Acts 26:1-8). Yet still there are many who are as sceptical as King Agrippa. Let us treat their scepticism with sympathy. It is very understandable. What, nevertheless, we are entitled to insist upon is that the New Testament is unequivocal in saying that Jesus was discovered to be alive when *everyone* was sure that he was dead. Now the entire New Testament may be an elaborate forgery. That is an arguable, if somewhat fanciful, proposition. It has been so argued in our own time. What is not legitimate is to admire the teaching of the 'Sermon on the Mount', to be moved by the story of the Crucifixion, and then to shelter from the challenge of the Resurrection by treating it as an illusion; on the ground that certain men and women could not bear to contemplate that all their hopes had proved false, and so they invented a story to give support to the illusion. That sceptical escape is intellectually disreputable. The qualitative testimony of the writings which we call the New Testament demands harder thinking than that.

The phrase 'a post-Resurrection collection' still calls for more consideration. Consider one very interesting fact to which full weight needs to be given. The whole Christian community of the first century was convinced that Jesus was alive after being dead. About that there is no dispute. Yet the men who collected all the material which we have in the four Gospels were so faithful to the facts that they make it crystal clear that, up until the *event* of the Resurrection, even those who were the most intimate companions of Jesus did not really understand him or his message. That is a very remarkable testimony to the authenticity of the narrative.

The companions of Jesus during his short ministry of three years, possibly only eighteen months, had indeed been profoundly attracted by him. Some were deeply devoted. But probably all of them lived with a vivid expectancy that he was the long looked for hope of his people, the man to liberate Israel from foreign rule. Even his inner circle thought and believed this right up until that devastating moment in the garden of Gethsemane when it did seem that all was lost and they all deserted him and ran away. Two of them, indeed, plucked up the courage to make a detour and arrived at the High Priest's house in time for the trial. But they did not make much of a showing even there. The Gospels are quite clear that until, after the Crucifixion, *something happened*, the disciples of Jesus hugged this political hope. How deeply ingrained it was can be seen by the response they made to what Jesus, *after* the Resurrection, taught about the meaning of the Kingdom of God. Even then, as Acts 1:6 has it, they asked if the moment had not arrived to 'establish once again the sovereignty of Israel?' How hard it is for a political dream to die! In the next chapter the author of Acts records a summary of a sermon by Peter, the man who only a few days before had flatly denied that he even knew Jesus, a desperate attempt at an alibi. That alibi and the sermon (Acts 2:22-36) take a lot of explanation unless, in between, *something happened*. The New Testament says that what happened was that God raised Jesus from the dead.

We will see in due course what the New Testament writers believed about God. That is very important, for only so will we understand what they came, in experience, to believe about Jesus. But for the present we may stay with that conviction that God raised Jesus from the dead. How it happened we do not know. But the result of what happened is historically as clear and beyond dispute as any event recorded since men learnt to write. The New Testament is there for anyone to read. What really does take a lot of explaining is that for nineteen hundred years an astonishing number of people drawn from every culture and class and race have, on reading the New Testament, been no less completely convinced that something did happen and that the New Testament is a reliable record of that happening, their confidence being based not just on the record but on their personal encounter with the living Jesus. The words about him have proved to be a living creature with hands and feet.

No less astonishing is the fact that all down the centuries there have been many who, having read the records and had the encounter, have been prepared to die for their conviction about both the records and the encounter. And there are many in our own day who have suffered and are still suffering for just this conviction. Curious, but true. No, this does not prove anything. It does not prove that the New Testament is a true record. But it ought to make anyone furiously to think.

But, there is still more to be drawn out from our phrase 'a post-Resurrection collection'. Another curious fact which will bear some thinking about is that, from immediately after the Resurrection, down to and including today, Christians who are serious about their Faith do, with relatively few exceptions, follow what they believe to be the wish of Jesus and meet together for one special common action. The earliest account comes in one of Paul's letters written to the Christians in Corinth about the year A.D. 55 (1 Cor. 11:23-26). Now the interesting fact is that from that account two convictions emerge. First, Christians are bidden to put themselves back in imagination into the Upper Room where on the night of his betrayal Jesus did four things. He took bread. He gave thanks over it. He broke it. He gave it to each one present. And very clearly he was understood to have identified himself in a special way with that four-fold action. The second conviction is that, from the earliest days, this symbolic action was understood as having to be continued until the Day when Jesus was to come again, an event in an unspecified future. What this means is that in that symbolic action it was recognised that in celebrating a *past* event and a *future* event Jesus was alive as a *present* event. Christians ever since have been quite convinced that, after some fashion beyond their understanding but not outside their experience, Jesus himself is *with* them and that by sharing in this action they are *with* Jesus. They share in his death and in his resurrection and await his 'coming again' in which they too will share. This is the Christian way of making the past and the future be present now, and it is all done in and through the Person of Jesus himself who, for the Christian, is the same yesterday, today, and for ever (Heb. 13:8). This is just one of the ways in which the New Testament asserts itself as a very contemporary book. It is a living book because it is about a living Person. The Jesus of history is a real Jesus, an historical personality. But he is not just an historical personality. We know him historically in so far as we know him today.

But, even now, we have by no means exhausted the inwardness of our phrase, 'a post-Resurrection collection'. We have seen that the collection was written with the unanimous conviction of all the authors that the Crucifixion was followed by the Resurrection. Yet, the testimony is quite clear that it was only after the Resurrection that the men and women who had been with Jesus really came to understand who he was and what was *some* of the meaning of what he had said and done. The word *some* is important. There is always new truth to be discovered about Jesus. Truths about Jesus never exhaust the Truth that is Jesus. That being noted as of paramount importance for Christian discipleship, it remains of the greatest interest that the things which he said during his ministry, now, after the Resurrection, being freshly understood, make it clear that Jesus himself thought of himself as being the message which he had been sent to deliver and not just as the messenger. This is confirmed when we turn to the four Gospels, remembering, as we must, that they embody the corporate memory not only of the eye-witnesses of his ministry but of all who, up till the time of writing, had proved on their own pulses the truth of what he had taught, the Truth he was.

The witness of Mark

Consider the Gospel of Mark, generally recognised as the earliest to have been written down, although the other Gospels contain material which is derived from independent traditions as early, if not earlier. In Mark from the very beginning we find Jesus saying 'The Kingdom of God is upon you' (1:15). And at once he calls men into a particular relationship with himself. They are to believe what he says, however much that may change their way of thinking. Mark's whole narrative is breath-taking in its sense of immediacy, in the speed at which it moves, as though everything depended on the right decision.

Mark clearly groups his material in order to emphasise this sense of the gravity of choice involved. And whether it be in his teaching, in his actions, or in controversy, he turns the spotlight on Jesus. It was Jesus himself who attracted attention, not so much by what he said as by the way he said it: not so much by what he did but by the way he did it. The focus is always on Jesus as being himself the Gospel. Quite deliberately Mark gives the superscription of his book – 'Here begins the Gospel of Jesus Christ'. The Good News is Jesus, and it 'must be proclaimed to all nations' (13:10).

The witness of Matthew

Matthew's record, which makes a great deal of use of Mark, also uses much independent material, some of which is also found in Luke. Matthew, as he looks back on the ministry of Jesus, clearly has a picture in his mind of Jesus as the great deliverer, the new Moses, but on a grander and more wonderful scale (24:14). Matthew is steeped in the tradition of his people for whom Moses was the effective spiritual founder of their nation. He was their law-giver and it was only by obedience to the law that the nation could hope for any future deliverance. This pattern determines the shape of the Gospel as Matthew interpreted it. More than anywhere else in the New Testament it is in this Gospel that the great principles of right living are laid down. And it is no accident that the teaching of Jesus is given an almost codified form in what is called the Sermon on the Mount. The great 'deliverance' that Moses made after his vigil on Mount Sinai finds its counterpart here in the great 'deliverance' which we find in Chapters 5, 6 and 7. A great utterance becomes a 'deliverance' in the fullest sense of the word when, in retrospect, it is seen to involve a demand, obedience to which issues in freedom. So it was with the 'deliverance' of the law of God on Mount Sinai. So Matthew interprets the law of Jesus. Both were utterly demanding and they still are, something we easily forget.

And equally easily we forget that the Sermon on the Mount is anything but a model of ethical instruction for the ordinary man, a programme fairly easy for the well-intentioned man to fulfil. Far otherwise. Its demand is for an ultimate and apparently impossible response. 'Be ye therefore perfect, even as your Father which is in heaven is perfect' (5:48 A.V.). Torrey has rendered this 'Be therefore all-including in your good-will, as your heavenly Father includes all.' A moment's intelligent reflection shows that the Sermon on the Mount is the most terrifying programme for living ever set before the human mind. It is an ultimate demand. But the same Gospel shows that there is a final succour available to the man and woman broken in spirit by their failure to reach this standard. And the final succour is Jesus himself, in his marvellous invitation – 'Come to me, all whose work is hard, whose load is heavy; and I will give you relief. Bend your necks to my yoke, and learn from me, for I am gentle and humble-hearted; and your souls will find relief. For my yoke is good to bear, my load is light' (11:28-30).

There is paradox here. The demand remains absolute, lest for one moment we allow ourselves any easy option when it comes to obedience to the demands of Jesus. But we are not confronted by an ethical demand. We are confronted by a person. And Matthew describes the person in the gracious words of Isaiah 42:3. 'He will not snap off the broken reed, nor snuff out the smouldering wick'; yet the context shows that the servant of whom Isaiah speaks is no less surely the judge (v.1) before whom all must stand. Absolute demand and final succour are reconciled in the person of Jesus himself. What is of great importance for our discipleship is that the invitation of Jesus — 'Come to me...' is in the context of the greatest claim that Jesus was remembered as having made for himself — 'Everything is entrusted to me by my Father; and no-one knows the Son but the Father, and no-one knows the Father but the Son and those to whom the Son may choose to reveal him.' (11:27)

As clearly as anywhere in the New Testament we have here the claim that the message is Jesus, that Jesus is the message — that he is the Great Commission — the revealer of God. Whoever wrote the Gospel, as we have it, knew that Jesus was continuing to reveal the Father, as he has been doing ever since. We can say with Michael Ramsey, lately Archbishop of Canterbury — 'God is Christlike and in him is no unchristlikeness at all'. To have received that revelation is to have entered into a particular relationship with the Great Commission. It is to know oneself commissioned.

The witness of Luke

The Gospel according to Luke adds a new dimension. The authors of the other three Gospels were certainly Jews, and there is little doubt that the sources upon which they drew were from traditions handed on by Christians who by birth were Jews. But Luke was a Gentile. Many Gentiles at that time were God-fearers, men and women who found their spiritual nourishment in attending the synagogue services and identifying themselves with the local Jewish community. Such may have been the Greeks who came to Jerusalem for the Passover and asked to see Jesus (John 12:20-21). Luke would certainly have been familiar with the Greek version of the Old Testament, the Septuagint. And the two books he wrote, Volume I, the Gospel, and Volume II, the Acts of the Apostles, unmistakably give us a sense of widening horizons. For Luke there is no doubt whatever that the Gospel is universal in its scope.

That the Gospel and the great commission were directed to all mankind finds a distinctive Lukan touch in that his genealogy of Jesus, as touching his humanity, is traced back to Adam, whereas Matthew stops at Abraham. The Angels' song at the Nativity, as Luke describes it, has no restrictive clauses. It is Luke who records the 'Alleluia' of Simeon as including all mankind. Again, whereas Matthew and Mark quote from Isaiah 40:3 only the words about a voice crying in the wilderness, Luke fills out the quotation to claim that the way which was to be prepared for the Lord was so designed that 'all flesh shall see it together' or as it has been rendered, 'all mankind shall see God's deliverance'. Only Luke gives the text of Jesus' first sermon, preached in Nazareth. It is at least striking that the text of that sermon stops where it does with the words 'the Lord's favour', and does not go on to refer to the 'vengeance of our God' which is what any Jewish audience in that day believed to be the lot of the Gentile world. Was the fact that Jesus paused there, the cause of some in the audience first becoming uneasy? Possibly. What is certain is that Luke found it most appropriate for his purpose in writing to Theophilus that Jesus, in interpreting his text, did in such forthright fashion show the mercy of God as extending beyond the limits of Israel to Naaman the Syrian, and to the widow woman of Sarepta in the territory of Sidon.

We do not know who Theophilus was, whether a believer or, in all likelihood, an enquirer. Judging by his Greek name he was a Gentile, and each of these little touches in the Gospel story, not to mention the Good Samaritan, would have found a grateful echo in that Gentile mind.

If, then, Chapter II of Matthew's Gospel can be explored as pointing to the very heart of the Great Commission himself, so in the last chapter of this Gospel Luke summarises his own understanding of that commission in Jesus' own words, as he opened the disciples' minds to understand the scriptures —

> This is what is written: that the Messiah is to suffer death and to rise from the dead on the third day, and that in his name repentance bringing the forgiveness of sins is to be proclaimed to all nations. Begin from Jerusalem: it is you who are the witnesses to all this. And mark this: I am sending upon you my Father's promised gift; so stay in this city until you are armed with power from above (24:46-49).

The Luke who wrote the Gospel is generally assumed to be the friend of Paul who, in one letter, refers to him as 'Luke the Physician'. What is very clear to any reader of these two volumes is that he was, in addition to being a doctor, also a supreme artist in words. The Gospel is full of unforgettable pictures. It was fitting that such an artist should be able to make the transition from Volume I to Volume II by the above quotation, where the accent falls on the word *begin*, and assumes that, once the promised gift is given, there will be a movement to the ends of the earth. This is picked up again at the beginning of Volume II.

The witness of Luke's Volume II

Here, in this second volume, the great artist appears in the full splendour of his creative power. The Book of the Acts of the Apostles can best be envisaged as a great fresco or a huge tapestry. We watch as one scene succeeds the next and, for the discerning eye, it is quite clear that the central figure is the Great Commission himself, and all the subordinate figures harmonise with him in proportion as they are themselves caught up into the same commission. What dominates this book is the fundamental conviction of the author that the message identified with the messenger is to be continuously proclaimed, and that in the very proclamation the Great Commission himself is present. But because Luke is dealing seriously with historical events he offers no simple picture of how the events unfolded. The apostles are no more idealised in the Acts of the Apostles than they are in the Gospels. Even after the Resurrection, even after the promised gift of his Father had been given, it is clear that those commissioned were still very far from certain as to what was to be involved for them in obeying it.

So our first glimpse of them is once again in that Upper Room where that unforgettable meal had been held, where the bread had been broken, where the wine had been blessed, and where a few days later they saw Jesus, crucified and risen. We need not think of the doors being fastened this time against the danger of arrest. We are told they were all praying together (1:14). But there is not much sense of movement. We see them still very preoccupied with the past. They seem to be trying to make sure that they have got the past under some kind of control. This is one possible, perhaps probable, reason for that rather strange episode of casting lots so as to find a successor to take the place of Judas, the Iscariot, now dead. The past was real. The future utterly obscure. But, at least, we see that they were waiting, though for what they did not know.

Then suddenly something else happened. Exactly what happened is not clear. Luke tries in words to communicate what words are not capable of expressing. But if we speak of men rushed off their feet with hearts aflame, all consumed with a tremendous certainty of a transforming power, we shall not be far from the spirit of the occasion. We will find ourselves almost compelled to say more, and use the words of Luke that, as he must later have been told by many of those who had been present, they knew that the promise of the Father had been given, knew that 'they were all filled with the Holy Spirit'.

Now the decisively important thing was the explanation given by Peter. Linking their new experience with an Old Testament prophecy, (Joel 2:28-29), he went on at once to focus attention upon Jesus — a Jesus who had been crucified and whom everyone in the crowd knew was dead. But Peter is uncompromising in his claim — 'This Jesus we speak of has been raised by God, as we can all bear witness. Exalted thus at God's right hand, he received the Holy Spirit from the Father, as was promised, and all that you now see and hear flows from him...this Jesus.' (See 2:14-41.)

Be it noted that the central message is Jesus and the hearers are bidden to 'accept as certain that God has made this Jesus, whom you crucified, both Lord and Messiah'. He is still addressing Jews, but in Luke's record of that occasion there comes, among Peter's 'many other words', the assurance that if they will indeed accept Jesus this gift of the Holy Spirit will be theirs also — 'For the promise is to you, and to your children, and to all who are far away, everyone whom the Lord our God may call' (2:39). In the afflatus of that moment Peter sees the future open. He was to have his moments of hesitation, of doubt, of compromise even, for Peter remained a very human being to the end. As with the rest of us the vision splendid can become strangely opaque. But Peter never lost it. The future was open.

Continuing our study of the great fresco, we see the sobering unfolding of events. And it must have been very sobering after all those people had been converted, three thousand in one day, to find that some had only jumped on the band-wagon of what seemed to be a popular movement, the latest sensation. This was not to be the last time that this has happened in history. Luke records the incident for our learning (5:1-11). But God in his mercy provides the best of all antidotes to superficiality — persecution.

As we move along the wall which carries our fresco we see a flogging (5:40): a trial scene and a judicial murder (6:8-8:1): then violent persecution. But at the centre of it all is Jesus. What happens after Peter and John have been flogged? '...the apostles went out from the Council rejoicing that they had been found worthy to suffer indignity for the sake of the Name. And every day they went steadily on with their teaching in the temple and in private houses, telling the good news of Jesus the messiah.' What happens at the end of the trial scene? Stephen 'sees' Jesus standing at the right hand of God, and, as he dies, he echoes the words which Jesus prayed as he was nailed to the Cross (7:55, 60). What happens as the sequel to violent persecution? Why, 'as for those who had been scattered, they went through the country preaching the Word' (8:4).

The commission is quite obviously being taken seriously. Men and women were still being rushed off their feet in more ways than one, their hearts on fire. Very prophetic of what has been happening all down history was one bit of early organisation. In order that the Apostles might be set free to get on with their commission, the Church was asked to choose some reliable men whose task it was to deal with details of administration — the kind of thing a good layman could do, like being secretary of the Parochial Church Council, or acting as treasurer. But it was all much too tidy! Organisation almost always is. There has, indeed, to be some but it must be the servant not the master in the life of the Church. It is at least remarkable that, of the seven men chosen to 'serve tables', do the administrative chores, two were snatched out almost at once for a quite different ministry. Stephen is called to witness by martyrdom. Philip makes the first break out into the wider world with his great evangelistic Mission in Samaria of all places! (8:4-13). And from there he sets off on a desert journey where he encounters the Ethiopian Chancellor of the Exchequer and is able so convincingly to interpret Isaiah 53 as being prophetic of Jesus that the Ethiopian is converted and baptised (8:26-40). Presumably the other five 'men of good reputation, full of the Holy Spirit and wisdom' had to do Stephen's and Philip's job as well as their own. Let there be no misunderstanding. To be full of the Holy Spirit and wisdom is just as much needed for the work of administration as it is for the work of preaching. What the early Christians had to learn, and what the Christians of later centuries have too often forgotten, is that pigeon-holing people into particular categories may not always best serve the purpose of the Great Commission.

We have seen how central Jesus was in the witness of
Stephen. It was the same with Philip. We are told quite simply
that 'he came down to a city in Samaria and began proclaiming
the Messiah to them'. We read that when they 'came to believe
Philip with his good news about the kingdom of God and the
name of Jesus Christ, they were baptised, men and women
alike' (8:5, 12). Had one of the women, not long before, met
Jesus at the well of Sychar? It may well have been so. It is a
characteristic of the Great Commission himself to be on the
ground first before his disciples arrive. And he is the same
today as he was then.

Somewhere along the fresco we are studying we arrive at a
scene which appears to be almost coincident with Philip's
missionary activities. Peter we are told was 'making a general
tour' (9:32) and found himself at Joppa. What a dramatic bit of
painting Luke does in his Chapter 10! We see a devout Gentile
soldier at his prayers. Suddenly the eyes of his mind, if we may
so put it, are almost blinded by a figure in shining robes. Was
the shining one Jesus incognito? Of course we cannot tell, but
it would be like him to have prepared Cornelius, just as, a few
miles away, he was preparing Peter, cautious, hesitating, honest
Peter. Peter had had his moment of vision on that unforgettable
day of Pentecost. He hadn't then been sure of what he meant
when, in the Spirit, he had spoken of 'all who are far away,
everyone whom the Lord our God may call'. But he probably
had some knowledge of Stephen's wide-ranging vision (7:48-
50) (echo, was it, of Jesus' own words to the woman at Sychar,
John 4:21-25?). And he had been down to Samaria to follow up
Philip's mission there. He would almost certainly have heard
of that desert encounter. He must have been doing a lot of
thinking. But he was still uncertain as to his direction. The
future was open, opening indeed in astonishing ways, but Peter
was cautious. We must not under-estimate the sincerity of his
caution. He had been devoted to Jesus but had proved again
and again that he was somewhat 'slow on the uptake'. Most of
us are like Peter in that. Anyway, Peter, hearing the improb-
able demand to break all the dietary rules upon which he had
been brought up, and to make a meal of unclean animals, and
being told not to be choosy (10:9-16), recognised the voice.
Thinking over this extraordinary experience he found himself

confronted with the invitation to visit a Gentile soldier in Caesarea. The penny dropped. And very soon we hear Peter telling Cornelius about Jesus. We have only a précis of what Peter said but it is clear that he was preaching the Gospel and that he did so with such power that there was a miniature Pentecost, there and then in that soldier's house.

Of course Peter had to explain himself when he got back to the Church in Jerusalem. Rumours had reached them of strange goings-on and of Peter being very much out of order, ritually and otherwise. It is all so easy to understand. Things were happening so fast and even the best of men could be forgiven for wondering what would happen next. For the moment, however, though only for the moment, Peter's explanation set their doubts at rest. We can hear the genuinely puzzled astonishment with which these Christians, all still devout Jews, almost gasped out the impossible idea — 'This means that God has granted life-giving repentance to the Gentiles also' (11:18).

Meanwhile the scattering of Christians through persecution had carried some of them as far as Phoenicia, Cyprus, and Antioch. We may suppose that most, if not all, of these were among those who had responded to the challenge of Peter's sermon on the day of Pentecost. They had stayed on in Jerusalem, had shared in that early experience of communal living, had daily attended the temple, had 'broken bread together' where they lodged, shared their simple meals with joy, met regularly to listen as the apostles told them more about Jesus; and learnt in a new way to pray together, (2:42-46). But they were far from home. Their intended stay in Jerusalem had only been to be there for the Feast. Now they found growing hostility. They could well be a serious embarrassment to their hosts and they had family responsibilities back home. So, as the author says, they were 'scattered abroad'.

The word for 'scattered' is the word from which the technical term for Jews living outside the home country is derived — *diaspora*. The same word is used in the first letter of Peter as describing those to whom he was writing. There is no reason to picture the scattering as a panic measure. What is quite certain is that these people on their way home told the good news of Jesus wherever they went. Quite clearly there was the beginning of a movement which was creating very serious anxiety among the Jewish leaders. After all, one reason for the Crucifixion of Jesus, the one which had satisfied the Roman authorities, was precisely that he was a centre of disaffection. It wasn't very long before we find a mob in one Roman colony protesting that these followers of Jesus were 'advocating customs which it is illegal for us Romans to adopt and follow' (16:21). Within weeks another mob in another city was complaining that these men 'who have made trouble all over the world have now come here... They all flout the Emperor's laws, and assert that there is a rival king, Jesus' (17:6-7). Something like a forest fire had started. Luke, on his fresco, can almost be seen etching in the flames just to show the link between what was happening everywhere and what had happened in Jerusalem on the day of Pentecost. And it all centred upon Jesus. Those commissioned had indeed begun in Jerusalem as instructed, and, as instructed, they had not stopped there.

A Roman citizen of Tarsus

Now comes the moment when Luke is going to spring his great surprise. He knows very well how greatly Theophilus would enjoy it, so the rest of the painting on his great fresco is devoted to this one theme. We have already seen how Philip was suddenly sent off on an apparently pointless journey along a desert road. We have seen Peter having a very uncomfortable and upsetting experience on a house-top in Joppa. We have heard the Christians in Jerusalem, the apostles and everyone else calling Peter to account, and somewhat guardedly welcoming the accession of a resident Gentile into the fellowship. But Jesus had already started on another journey leading this time to the world's end. Jesus is always ahead. He is there to meet us, just as he was waiting outside Damascus when a man called Saul was hurrying with a police escort to search the Jewish colony in Damascus for his followers.

Acres of newsprint have been covered to explain what happened on the Jerusalem–Damascus road at noon one day possibly in the year A.D. 32. (This date has been carefully argued by W.M. Ramsay in his *Pauline and Other Studies*) But the date is not important. What happened to Saul, a devout

Jew, and also by birth a Roman citizen, was Jesus. Luke reports the incident three times, on each occasion underlining its real significance. Whatever the variety of wording in Luke's three reports, two of them being records of speeches made by Paul (Acts 9:15, 22:21, 26:17) to different audiences, the salient fact is clear. Paul has been commissioned to break bounds. And, while taking every opportunity to speak to his fellow-countrymen, he recognises a particular calling to the world outside the covenant of God's promises, as the Jewish people, and he himself hitherto, had understood them.

The witness of Paul

Later in his letters Paul is quite explicit about his commission. In what may well be the first letter that he wrote, the one to the Galatians, he puts his call with dramatic simplicity: 'in his good pleasure God, who had set me apart from birth and called me through his grace, chose to reveal his Son to me and through me, in order that I might proclaim him among the Gentiles' (Gal. 1:15-16). Later in a greatly expanded version of his argument with the Galatians, itself a key document to anyone who would understand the gospel, Paul writes to the Romans about the gospel which 'is about Jesus Christ our Lord', and goes on at once to say, 'Through him I received the privilege of a commission in his name to lead to faith and obedience men in all nations, yourselves among them' (1:4-6).

Luke has two other touches on his fresco, apart from describing Paul's missionary journeys, touches which are worth pondering. The first is, on any reckoning, quite remarkable. On his first journey as a missionary Paul is in the city of Antioch in Pisidia. We have a long account of his stay (Acts 13) and of the very considerable impact which he made, particularly on the Gentiles in his various audiences. Then come these startling words: 'The Lord commanded us, saying, I have set thee to be a light of the Gentiles, that thou shouldst be for salvation unto the ends of the earth' (v. 47 A.V.). This is worth close study. Paul takes directly to himself the words of Isaiah 49:6, words originally addressed to God's people Israel. It is an audacious claim, but also a subtle appeal, for being himself an Israelite he is appealing to the Jews in his audience to recognise God's intended missionary destiny for his chosen people. Even more striking is the fact that we have here an echo of the hymn of praise by old Simeon (Luke 2:32). That was surely no accidental slip of the artist's brush! And that hymn of praise was directed by Simeon to the child Jesus resting in his arms. The Great Commission and his commissioned followers are one. (See Matt. 10:40, Mark 3:35, Gal. 2:20.)

There is a final touch as Luke reaches the end of his fresco, the last scene in his vast tapestry. We see Paul making a last appeal to his fellow-countrymen to rise to their destiny. The appeal fails. 'Take notice,' says Paul, 'that this salvation of God has been sent to the Gentiles: the Gentiles will listen' (28:28). Those last words are surely also a subtle appeal to Theophilus. It is difficult to believe that the two volumes by this consummate artist failed to carry conviction to their first reader. They have certainly had a remarkable convincing power ever since.

Luke, the first of many hundreds of biographers of Paul, has left us in no doubt that it was Paul who first fully understood the Great Commission himself and what was involved in being united with his will and purpose. Something of what Paul had understood we have already seen, but in his letters he gives us more pieces of self-revelation which must be noted.

The witness of Paul's correspondence

Perhaps the most poignant of all Paul's letters is that to the Galatians. Here were the first-fruits of his earliest missionary undertaking, and he quickly saw that news he had heard from Galatia meant that the gospel was at stake. Dramatically, we see how Paul's profoundly affectionate nature could burst into flaming anger at what he felt was a betrayal of the gospel, and that betrayal at the hands of fellow-Christians. It is one of the melancholy facts of history that from the first there were Christians whose God was too small, whose gospel was too limited. It was out of the white heat of his indignation that there came Paul's splendid declaration — 'There is no such thing as Jew and Greek, slave and freeman, male and female; for you are all one person in Christ Jesus' (Gal. 3:28).

In quieter mood, though scarcely less anxious, he says the same thing in one of his last letters near the end of his life when he writes to the Christians in Colossae (3:11). But it is in his long letter to the Christians in Rome that he expands his vision. Chapters 9-11 are in fact that expansion, with the heart of it in Chapter 10:11-15. 'Everyone who invokes the name of the Lord will be saved. How could they invoke one in whom they had no faith? And how could they have faith in one they had never heard of? And how hear without someone to spread the news? And how could anyone spread the news without a commission to do so?'

What that commission meant in practice to Paul is summed up in his great definition of how he understood the nature of his task, a definition he gives us in his first letter to the Corinthians.

I have made myself every man's servant, to win over as many as possible. To Jews I became like a Jew, to win Jews; as they are subject to the law of Moses, I put myself under that law to win them although I am not myself subject to it. To win Gentiles, who are outside the law, I made myself like one of them, although I am not in truth outside God's law, being under the law of Christ. To the weak I became weak, to win the weak. Indeed, I have become everything in turn to men of every sort, so that in one way or another I may save some. All this I do for the sake of the Gospel, to bear my part in proclaiming it (9:19-23).

What is the gospel?

In a much later letter he was to quote an early Christian hymn which shows exactly where he found the pattern for his missionary practice. It is clearly set out in Philippians 2:5-11. Paul makes very few references to the earthly ministry of Jesus but that passage shows that he had discovered its central meaning. If ever a man understood the majesty and range of the gospel it was Paul. And because he understood it it was unthinkable not to proclaim it (1 Cor. 9:16).

What was this gospel? We have seen, in the memoirs telling

about Jesus which we know by the names of Matthew and Mark and Luke, that Jesus himself is the message as well as the messenger. It is crystal clear that before these books were written Paul had already expressed what was the conviction of the Christians who had companied with Jesus in his ministry, had witnessed the Crucifixion, had been decisively changed into new men and women by his Resurrection, and were living in union with him. No reader of his letters can have any doubt of this. But no careful reader will make the mistake, which has sometimes been made, that Paul was the real founder of Christianity. Luke may well have found in Paul the confidence to describe the ministry of Jesus as he did, though even he does not quote Paul in doing so. Matthew and Mark and to a large extent Luke, also, are drawing on quite independent sources. Paul is emphatic that his gospel is something which he has *accepted* at the hands of others but has *proved* in his own experience. (See Gal. 1:18-19, 2:1-10; Rom. 1:2-6; 1 Cor. 2:1, 3:1-13, 11:23-26, 15:1-7, 11; Eph. 2:20, 4:20-21; Col. 1:23, 2:6-8, 1 Thess. 2:13; 2 Thess. 2:15 — part of the evidence from Paul himself that he was not inventing a message but passing it on.)

This is what he had proved in his own experience, something he had in common with his fellow-Christians. Most intimately he expresses it in Galatians 2:20 — 'I have been crucified with Christ: the life I now live is not my life, but the life which Christ lives in me; and my present bodily life is lived by faith in the Son of God, who loved me and sacrificed himself for me.'

At the very centre of Paul's gospel are three facts — the Cross, the Resurrection, and the indwelling Christ. It is the central purpose of all Paul's letters — and indeed of all the correspondence which occupies so much of the New Testament, not only the letters written by Paul — to testify to these facts. Indeed the whole New Testament was written to stress this three-fold experience. It is what the four Gospels are concerned to define as being the real meaning of Jesus. One quarter of the Gospel of Matthew; one third of the Gospel of Mark; one quarter of the Gospel of Luke; nearly half of the Gospel of John are concerned with the immediate events leading up to the Crucifixion, the Resurrection and the assurance of the indwelling presence of Jesus. That alone is striking evidence of how profoundly convinced were the Christians of the first century that herein lay the Good News which they were commissioned to proclaim.

Now it is Paul who devoted most attention to drawing out the meaning of this three-fold experience. And while at one place in his argument he may lay his stress on the Cross, at another on the Resurrection, at yet another on the indwelling Christ, yet they must never be separated as though one of them in particular represents the gospel. All too many Christians have been tempted to do just this. Some have taken a single verse, for instance 1 Corinthians 2:2 'I resolved that while I was with you I would think of nothing but Jesus Christ — Christ nailed to the Cross' and have made that the whole gospel. Some have even suggested that Paul was so resolved because, so they claim, he had realised that his witness to the gospel in Athens, from where he had come to Corinth, had been a failure (Acts 17:16-34). What a curious misunderstanding, for on that occasion, as we are told, some men joined him and became believers, including Dionysius, a member of the Court of Areopagus; also a woman named Damaris, and others besides. How many preachers can claim as many conversions after a single address? And on what authority can anyone say that in talking about Jesus, Paul, on that single occasion, failed to mention the Cross? What happened in that Athenian audience was that they were struck by the incredible message of a man being raised from the dead. There was nothing new about a crucifixion. But resurrection was News. They were so excited that they even thought that *Anastasis*, the Greek word for resurrection, was meant to be spelt with a capital A, as being another God alongside Jesus!

All the evidence of Paul's letters is that he kept the proportion of the gospel — Cross, Resurrection, Indwelling. Let us be clear and gladly clear that we cannot fashion a simple interpretation of this gospel and say that the cross meant *just* this, that the Resurrection meant *just* that and nothing else, that the indwelling Christ must be understood in only one way. The wonder of the grace of God is set out for us as clearly as anywhere in Paul's letter to the Romans, Chapters 5 and 6, though even to say that is to invite immediate queries from those who have been overwhelmed by the argument of Romans, Chapters 3 and 4. Yet again, how many have found themselves in Chapters 7 and 8 and live there rejoicingly? What all can echo is 1 Corinthians 1:30-31 — 'You are in Christ Jesus by God's act, for God has made him our wisdom; he is our righteousness; in him we are consecrated and set free.' How wonderful that we can all share in that lyrical outburst in 2 Corinthians 5:17-20—

> When anyone is united to Christ, there is a new world; the old order has gone, and a new order has already begun. From first to last this has been the work of God. He has reconciled us men to himself through Christ, and he has enlisted us in this service of reconciliation. What I mean is, that God was in Christ reconciling the world to himself, no longer holding men's misdeeds against them, and that he has entrusted us with the message of reconciliation. We come therefore as Christ's ambassadors. It is as if God was appealing to you through us; in Christ's name, we implore you, be reconciled to God.

Perhaps it is worth remembering that here, and in all his letters, Paul is writing to Christians. But Paul never doubts for a moment that they are also sinners, as is Paul himself. We have been saved: we are continually being saved: we will be saved. That is Paul's doctrine of assurance. Nevertheless this is no easy salvation. In Paul there is no cheap grace. This lyrical passage passes straight into a baffling mystery — 'Christ was innocent of sin, and yet for our sake God made him one with the sinfulness of men, so that in him we might be made one with the goodness of God himself' (v.21).

We are standing in the darkness of the Cross. There is only one place and one atttitude in which even an attempt at a doctrine of the Atonement should be made — that is on one's knees in that darkness. It is a pity that so much has been written about the Atonement in broad daylight! But, Paul was right. It is out of darkness that the light shines and it was out of darkness that God 'caused his light to shine *within* us, to give the light of revelation — the revelation of the glory of God in the face of Jesus Christ' (2 Cor. 4:6). To say this is not to decry the working out of a theology or to underestimate the important ministry of those called to this task. This book is in debt to countless theologians. It is itself an essay in theology, but in so far as it, or any theology, trespasses far from the mystery of God and his revelation it will be bad theology.

The witness of John

There is a fourth Gospel at which we have not yet looked, the one we know as the Gospel of John. Here is a portrait of Jesus quite unlike the ones which we have in Matthew and Mark and Luke. It reads like the meditations of a life-time by a man whose whole being was absorbed in seeking to understand Jesus, and then to interpret to others what in his experience he had discovered. This was certainly a disciple who had proved in his own life what it meant to 'abide', to dwell with Jesus, to think his thoughts after him, and from continual thinking to see what was the real inner meaning of the many sayings of Jesus which had been handed down by the other Gospel writers, and indeed by what he also knew of the experience of the Christian Church.

There had come a moment in the last hours of Jesus' earthly life when, in talking with his friends, he had told them about Another who was to be sent by his heavenly Father, one whom Jesus called 'the Spirit of truth', who was to be the breath of God to inspire the friends of Jesus. Here again we are on the edge of mystery. It is very very difficult to put a living experience into words. In the New Testament we see different writers trying to do just this and using quite different words to do it. The one certain way to be mistaken is to take one of these expressions as adequate and to dismiss the others. So it was that John remembered something of what Jesus had said about the Other—

There is still much that I could say to you, but the burden would be too great for you now. However, when he comes who is the Spirit of truth, he will guide you into all the truth; for he will not speak on his own authority, but will tell only what he hears; and he will make known to you the things that are coming. He will glorify me, for everything that he makes known to you he will draw from what is mine. All that the Father has is mine, and that is why I said 'everything that he makes known to you he will draw from what is mine.' (16:12-15)

That was the proved experience of John. Paul is recording the same experience in different words when, after quoting Isaiah 64:4 — 'Things beyond our seeing, things beyond our hearing, things beyond our imagining, all prepared by God for those who love him' — he added, 'these it is that God has revealed to us through the Spirit' (1 Cor. 2:9-10). We are here trembling on the edge of understanding the real meaning of inspiration which is something personal, an awareness of Another, who brings our minds alive in a new way, making them acutely sensitive to what is happening around us. In the Old Testament the men who had this experience said quite simply, 'Thus saith the Lord', or 'The Lord hath spoken'. Paul can make the tremendous claim, 'we possess the mind of Christ' (1 Cor. 2:16). It is that mind which John is seeking to interpret. There is no contradiction between the Jesus of the Fourth Gospel and the Jesus of the other three Gospels. We have already seen how, in Chapter 11 of Matthew's Gospel (v. 27), Jesus speaks of his intimacy with his Father in heaven. John develops this as the main theme of his testimony to what he has come to see Jesus meant in all his living and speaking and dying. And there is no contradiction between John and Paul. We could indeed say that John's Gospel is a wonderful expansion of one single sentence of Paul's — 'God was in Christ reconciling the world to himself' (2 Cor. 5:19). That is but another way of describing the word of Jesus recorded by John 'I shall draw all men to myself, when I am lifted up from the earth' (12:32). And, lest there be any doubt as to what that meant, John adds 'This he said to indicate the kind of death he was to die'. Another Gospel, that of Mark, records Jesus as saying that the Son of Man did not come to be served but to serve, and to surrender his life as a ransom for many. In the New Testament there is one book other than the letter to the Romans, which might fairly be called a sustained theological argument, the Letter to the Hebrews.

Its central theme is that of all the New Testament and is summarised in the words, 'In Jesus...we do see one who for a short while was made lower than the angels, crowned now with glory and honour because he suffered death, so that, by God's gracious will, in tasting death he should stand for us all' (2:9).

Those words — 'stand for us all' are a continual refrain in the New Testament. In awe-inspiring vision we see, with John, that at the heart of the universe itself, that incredible mystery 'life' is so related to Jesus that it can be said that, 'All that came to be was alive with his life' (1:4). To his friend Thomas, who is greatly puzzled by the thought of Jesus dying, Jesus says quite simply, 'I am life' (14:6). He had said the same words to a sorrowing friend in her bereavement only a few weeks before (11:25). For John the mystery of the universe and the mystery of each one of us is directly linked with Jesus. Is it any wonder that his whole Gospel is an act of worship, a demand for worship? It is no accident that it is in his Gospel that we hear that same troubled Thomas exclaiming to the risen Jesus, 'My Lord and my God.'

This brings us to a point of outstanding importance. In those words Thomas is only articulating the response of the first Christians who, in the light of the Resurrection and with the experience of continuing fellowship with the living Jesus, and the power for living with which that fellowship endued them, should come, not suddenly, but surely to the conviction that Christ was 'God's own proof of his love towards us' (Rom. 5:8). If, indeed, God was reconciling the world to himself by Christ (2 Cor. 5:19 margin), then worship was the only possible response of the man who knew himself to be reconciled.

Letting God be God

Now these men who thought like this and reached this conclusion were devout Jews. Gentiles might have reached the same conclusion by a much easier path. In their myths God was frequently discovered in human form. Not so with the Jews. For them their long history is the story of a continuing struggle towards a right understanding of the nature and character of the God they worshipped. If it is true of the people of the New Covenant that they must work out their own salvation in fear and trembling, as Paul says in his letter to the Philippians (2:12). If they had to remember that it is God who is working in them 'inspiring both the will and the deed, for his own chosen purpose', this is no less true of the people of the Old Covenant. They had to learn a great deal about God and God took a long time and was very patient in teaching them. The people of the Old Covenant were just as primitive and cultured as the people round them, neither more nor less, and their ideas about God and how he worked needed continual refining. The refining fires of God's revelation in the events of their history drew an obedient response from many of their most sensitive leaders. They were brought by God to such a right judgement about him that in due course some were able to recognise 'the glory of God in the face of Jesus Christ' (2 Cor. 4:6) and transmit that recognition as being the heart of the gospel.

There is a remarkable continuity in the long history of religion. Perhaps the earliest designation of God in the Old Testament is a word which signifies that almighty power which appears to be at work all through the natural world. That was a true insight, however primitively conceived, and it is substantially common to all men everywhere. As to its continuity, as an expression of reality, it is intriguing to find that of the 91 Collects provided in the 1662 Book of Common Prayer, both for Sundays, other holy days and the feasts of major saints, no less than 46 are addressed to 'Almighty God' and at least 6 more have the idea of God's power explicitly stated. No doubt by 1662, and long before that, the idea of God as almighty had been redefined in the light of Jesus, so that, as the daily morning collect has it, this almighty God is 'our heavenly Father'; yet there remains the certainty that in so addressing him we are addressing the One who is in control of human destiny no less than of the natural order.

Between the time of Moses and that of Elijah we find vividly presented in the Old Testament the continual struggle to find, on the one hand, a convenient local god to whom appeal can be made, and on the other hand to acknowledge the one and only God. This is a perennial problem in all human experience and is just as much a real human predicament today as it was when, to use the fierce language of Israel's prophets, the people went a-whoring after the Baalim of the local cults. Dramatically, Elijah insists that only One can be God, Yahweh or Baal. The inescapability of choice becomes a central fact of prophetic religion.

But the one whom Elijah insisted upon as being the only God was already, at least from the time of Moses, understood as being one of whom it was good news to know his strange name, 'I am that I am'; one who is truly present, ready to help and to act, as he had always been, the God who had revealed himself to Abraham, to Isaac and to Jacob (Exod. 3:1-15).

Very easily the belief became current that just because this God was so obviously concerned with the people of Israel he could be comfortably assumed to be a national possession, the one whose obligations to his people were as real as their obligations to him. This was a profound error and the great prophets of Israel were deeply concerned to correct this illusion. Yet within the comforting illusion there was a profound truth, however misinterpreted. This God who was so concerned with the details of the national life and with all the relationships between men, came to be recognised as a God who had to be understood in a personal way. He was seen to be one with whom a personal relationship was possible. The Psalms and the book of Jeremiah are eloquent of this deep and true understanding.

Yet still there was more for the people of the Old Covenant to learn. If there really was only one God then he was the God of all the nations, not only of Israel. The *beginning* of the realisation of this is clearly expressed in Isaiah 52:7-10 (R.S.V.)

How beautiful upon the mountains are the feet of him who brings good tidings, who publishes peace, who brings good tidings of good, who publishes salvation, who says to Zion, 'Your God reigns'. Hark, your watchmen lift up their voice, together they sing for joy; for eye to eye they see the return of the Lord to Zion. Break forth together into singing, you waste places of Jerusalem; for the Lord has comforted his people, he has redeemed Jerusalem. The Lord has bared his holy arm before the eyes of all the nations; and all the ends of the earth shall see the salvation of our God.

That is still a limited vision which sees an almost exclusive significance in Jerusalem and in the people of Israel. There is, of course, a truth in that limited vision. Much later Paul will insist that the people of Israel do have a special place in the purpose of God, and he will quote a parallel passage (Isa. 49:6), though giving it a much more inclusive emphasis. For Paul finds in the prophets of Israel a foretaste of what he is sure is implied in the gospel. The God who has entrusted him with the gospel is the God who had first entrusted the people of Israel with a responsibility which was to be as wide as the world. It is one of the high moments of inspired insight when the prophet Zechariah can see that 'the Lord shall become King over all the earth; on that day the Lord shall be one Lord and his name the one name' (14:9). The implication of that vision, not easily accepted then or now, is that 'the God who made the world and everything in it...gives to all men life and breath and everything. And he made from one every nation of men to live on all the face of the earth...' And Paul goes on to insist that this God is 'not far from each one of us' (Acts 17:24-27 R.S.V.). In this context he tells of Jesus and the reality of his living presence.

That there is only one God, that in the universe there is only one point of moral reference to which men must attend, carries with it the essential unity of mankind. It is the great heritage of this conviction which lies at the root of what the New Testament understands by the word, *God*. And it was this which Jesus was always proclaiming in and through what he was, in and through what he said, in and through how he died, in and through his victory over death. It is this view of God which can be claimed to be the gospel of the Old Testament, a gospel clothed in flesh and blood in the person of Jesus who is the gospel of the New Testament — not two gospels but one. The Bible is a library with this fundamental theme.

The forgiveness of God

There is tragedy enough in the Bible, in all conscience; the tragedy of a chosen people failing fully to understand why they were chosen. And the New Testament is equally frank about the failure of the disciples of Jesus to understand the reason for their calling. Subsequent history is, on any account, sober reading particularly in so far as it records the activities and inactivities of the Church. Yet the Bible from start to finish has as its central theme the forgiveness of God. And in Jesus that forgiveness found unique expression. If one sentence can sum up Christian experience it is the words which come in 1 John 2:1-2 — 'Jesus...is himself the remedy for the defilement of our sins, not our sins only but the sins of all the world'. That is what the gospel is about and why it has to be proclaimed to all the world.

But the gospel is more even than that. One of the most wonderful and humbling experiences of human life is the discovery that scarcely has one asked forgiveness for some quite deliberate sin, some choice of evil in preference to the good, than one finds oneself trusted by God, entrusted with some new task, some new responsibility for which one would have imagined oneself disqualified by the betrayal of that trust in the sin just committed. Anyone who has had this experience as one of the miracles of the life of discipleship knows the thrill of the gospel. In the letter to the Ephesians this finds vivid description in Chapter 3:7-9. To anyone who has in this way discovered 'the unfathomable riches of Christ' (v.9) there is no doubt of his having been put in trust with the gospel.

This is the all-sufficient reason why any follower of Jesus can know himself to be, prospectively, included, in that Upper Room on the evening of the first Easter day, to hear for himself the blessing and the commission: 'Peace be with you. As the Father sent me, so I send you'; to experience for himself the assurance of power, 'receive the Holy Spirit'; to become everyone's debtor with the charge, 'If you forgive any man's sins, they stand forgiven; if you pronounce them unforgiven, unforgiven they remain' (John 20:21-23).

The forgiveness of man

That occasion in the Upper Room, we may, in all reverence, insist, involves no selective offering of 'the power of the keys'. To refuse by neglect to share the wonder of forgiveness with others is very effectively to 'pronounce them unforgiven'. It is an awful responsibility for any Christian to take lightly the forgiveness of God. To neglect to share it with others is to reduce the prayer our Lord taught us to nothing but a muttered ritual, unrelated to living. To be careless about those who do not know Jesus and what he has done for us and all mankind is to raise very seriously the question whether we really know him at all. In that short letter described as 'The First Letter of John' the issue is posed with terrifying simplicity:

> The man who does not love is still in the realm of death, for everyone who hates his brother is a murderer, and no murderer, as you know, has eternal life within him. It is by this that we know what love is: that Christ laid down his life for us. And we in our turn arc bound to lay down our lives for our brothers. But if a man has enough to live on, and yet when he sees his brother in need shuts up his heart against him, how can it be said that the divine love dwells in him? My children, love must not be a matter of words or talk; it must be genuine, and show itself in action (1 John 3:14-18).

From that passage it is clear that Christians are not individuals, bent on a mere individual salvation. They are members one of another. They are, as the New English Bible has it, 'incorporate in Christ Jesus' (Eph. 1:1, Phil. 1:1, Col. 1:2). But the words of the passage just quoted must be given a far wider context. Jesus had laid down a universal principle which fully justifies the contrast of 'hate' and 'love' which seem so stark (Matt. 5:38-48). And he had told about a man who fell among thieves, a stranger, an alien, a man of another creed. Neglect of the duty of love to others possesses the quality of murder. Such neglect raises a fundamental question about our own share in eternal life. This is high doctrine and very uncomfortable indeed. There is a true sense in which no Christian has any right ever to feel comfortable as long as there are any anywhere who do not know Christ.

The Great Commission, when he passed on his commission, certainly intended it to be corporately, no less than individually, expressed. This is what Paul saw so clearly, and described in the startling phrase 'The Body of Christ'. This 'Body' as he shows in 1 Corinthians 12 and in other places is essentially corporate without in any way reducing the individual responsibility of each of the individual members. But he is clear that the Great Commission uses each of us according to our gifts. Something of the variety of the Christian life can be gleaned from that same chapter (vs. 27-30). And the following chapter 13 vividly complements the challenge of 1 John 3:14-18. Many other passages underline the variety of discipleship.

If the passage from 1 John 3:14-18 is a controlling test of discipleship then it is clear that while speaking, in all its varied forms of preaching and teaching and exhortation, has its indispensable place in the corporate witness, there is another kind of witness which has no less decisive a place in the evangelistic outworking of the great commission. Again, the New Testament is replete with illustrations. Here a Concordance is of particular value. Young's great Concordance gives the A.V. references for words like 'walk', 'witness', 'testimony', 'confession'. So does Cruden's Concordance. And there is also one for the Revised Standard Version. 1 Corinthians 14:23-33, 2 Corinthians 9:13, and 1 Peter 2:11-12 are three examples of the way in which witness is possible for every Christian, whatever his gifts, or apparent lack of gifts, may be.

There is an intriguing passage at the end of Paul's letter to the Christians in Philippi where Paul says that all God's people in Rome 'especially those of Caesar's household' (4:22 R.S.V.) send their greetings with his. There are no convincing reasons against believing that Paul wrote this in Rome. How had the gospel penetrated to 'Caesar's household'? The centurion and the soldiers who had seen Paul in action on that dangerous voyage described in Acts chapters 27 and 28, who had wintered with him in Malta, could hardly have failed to talk about this brave man. Earlier still, there was that centurion in Caesarea, a member of a cohort consisting of soldiers from Italy settled in Syria. They could have had friends in Rome. Was this indirectly Peter's first contribution to the foundation of the Christian community in Rome? Perhaps more likely still was the soldier of the Praetorian guard who was chained to Paul, a duty of intolerable drudgery, enlivened, perhaps, by the coming and going of visitors, the puzzling correspondence continually being dictated, and the personality of Paul himself. Can one, for a moment, imagine Paul not by all means trying to save each successive soldier who had this particularly irksome 'fatigue'? In all these ways the gospel could have entered 'Caesar's household'. And there may have been other ways more unlikely still. In his imaginative reconstruction of the Rome of Nero's time F.W. Farrar, on what authority I do not know, claims that Claudia Acte, a favourite mistress of the Emperor himself, was a Christian. A much more recent work of imagination, Naomi Mitchison's *The Blood of the Martyrs*, also speaks of this same Claudia Acte as a mistress of Nero, and very much a member of the inner circle of that household. There was nothing impossible about this in that first-century world.

More intriguing still, and what at least is certain, is that the phrase 'Caesar's household' was commonly used to denote the Roman civil service, all those responsible for the administration of the Roman Empire, wherever they might be. No doubt but that a number of such men must have been involved in the proceedings about Paul. His more than two years living there in Rome in a hired house (Acts 28:30) must have provided ample opportunity for a great many civil servants, as well as soldiers, to have got to know Paul. And to know Paul was quite certainly to come face to face with Jesus Christ. So

> Even amongst those who ruled and administered the empire of Rome there were Christians. There is hardly any sentence which shows more how Christianity had infiltrated even into the highest positions in the empire. It was to be another three hundred years before Christianity became the religion of the empire, but already the first signs of the ultimate triumph of Christ were to be seen. The crucified Galilean carpenter had already begun to rule those who ruled the greatest empire in the world.

Such is William Barclay's conclusion in his Daily Study Bible Commentary on Philippians.

Our study of the New Testament evidence about the Great

Commission must be completed, as far as space allows, with a candid review of the *exclusive* demand which the commission made, and also the *inclusive* intention with which it was communicated. Only if these are held together and always interpreted in the light of what we know of the Great Commission himself, will we possess a yardstick by which to arrive at some evaluation of the long history of the Christian Mission. Then we may be in a position to review with understanding the variant forms under which the great commission is being interpreted today.

The *exclusive* demand

There is something unaccommodating about monotheism, whatever be the way in which the mystery of the Divine unity is understood. 'Hear, O Israel, the Lord our God is one Lord' (Deut. 6:4 R.S.V.), 'You shall have no other gods before me' (Exod. 20:3 R.S.V.). This is the fundamental assertion of Hebrew faith, affirmed by its great law-giver, Moses. It is the constant refrain of the great prophets 'I am God, there is no other' (Isa. 46:9). And it was a confidence of prophetic faith that someday this would be recognised by all the world. 'The Lord shall become king over all the earth; on that day the Lord shall be one Lord and his name the one name' (Zech. 14:9). From one point of view the whole of the Old Testament is the record of a tremendous struggle to make this affirmation the rule of faith and action.

Jesus is no less demanding. At the beginning of his public ministry, in the hour of his great testing as to where his loyalty stood, he says: 'You shall worship the Lord your God and him only shall you serve' (Matt. 4:10 R.S.V.). He reaffirms Deuteronomy 6:4 when asked which is the greatest commandment, 'Hear, O Israel: the Lord our God, the Lord is one' (Mark 12:29 R.S.V.). For him the Father in heaven is 'Lord of heaven and earth' (Matt. 11.25). His whole teaching about God as Father assumes that there can be no other than he. And it is because he identifies his own will completely with that of the Father in heaven that he can make the exclusive claim, 'I am the way; I am the truth and I am life; no-one comes to the Father except by me' (John 14:6). In that most revealing prayer recorded in John 17, once overheard hard to be forgotten, he says, 'This is eternal life: to know thee who alone art truly God' (John 17:3). That is no more than an affirmation of everything he had taught by his life and by his lips. The Gospels are entirely unanimous about what Jesus taught about God.

These Gospels summarise the truth as Jesus proclaimed it, as it had been handed down by oral tradition in the first and second generation after the Resurrection. What is quite clear is that the same exclusive demand is there in the apostolic preaching from the very beginning. Peter, speaking very much *ad hominem* to a critical audience of Jews (Acts 3:22) recalls to their memories a curious prophecy attributed to Moses that God 'will raise up for you a prophet like me from among you, from your brethren — him you shall heed' (Deut. 18:15 R.S.V.). And then in very uncompromising mood, expressing his urgency, he goes on to quote from Leviticus 23:29, which speaks of the Day of Atonement, the need for everyone to treat its solemnity seriously, and adds that whoever does not take the Day seriously is to be 'cut off from his people'. That, by the way, is an intriguing side-light on the possibility that, even at so early a date in their understanding of Jesus, the disciples saw in him the Atonement. Much later, Peter wrote a letter in which he could say that 'Christ also died for our sins once and for all' (1 Peter 3:18), a text which has ever since been held to be central to a Christian understanding of the Cross.

No wonder, then, that the same Peter can declare, 'There is no salvation in anyone else at all, for there is no other name under heaven granted to men, by which we may receive salvation' (Acts 4:12).

Paul is no less clear that the gospel which he has been commissioned to proclaim 'is the saving power of God for everyone who has faith' (Rom. 1:16). If possible, in even more striking fashion, he sees Christ as the very source of a new creation, a present reality which anticipates the new heaven and the new earth at the end of time (2 Cor. 5:17). Here is a demand on faith which is as exclusive as that immensely solemn statement in 1 John 5:12 — 'He who possesses the Son has life indeed; he who does not possess the Son of God has not that life.'

Enough has been said to show how basic to the New Testament is the conviction that the universe has only one centre — God — known as Father, made visible in Jesus, experienced in the Holy Spirit, not three Gods but one God and to be obeyed as such. For the Christian, God is as much to be known as One as to any Jew, however much that unity is understood by Christians to contain a mystery which practical experience in living has justified. That mystery has been formulated in the doctrine of the Trinity, which is the Christian doctrine of the unity of God.

The other great monotheistic religion, Islam, is also as exclusive as the other two in its demand on man's allegiance. Every morning the Muslim, if he hears the Muezzin's call, hears the witness 'There is no God but God.' Repeatedly, the Qur'an refers to God as Al-Wahid — the One. The Surah of Unity (Surah 112), by tradition one of the very earliest of the revelation received by Muhammad, reads,

He is God alone, God the Eternal (undivided)
He does not beget and He is not begotten
There is none coequal with Him.

One distinguished Christian scholar of Islam, Dr. Kenneth Cragg, believes that this Surah must go back even before Muhammad had had occasion to meet the enquiries of Jews and Christians as to his doctrine of God. He adds that this Surah 'is held to be worth a third of the whole Qur'an and the seven heavens and the seven earths are founded upon it. To confess this verse, a tradition affirms, is to shed one's sins as a man might strip a tree in autumn of its leaves'.

That is exclusive enough in all conscience. Such is the essence of monotheism. And it is an inevitable sequel that, under heaven, mankind is no less one. To affirm the unity of mankind, as transcending all divisions of race and class, or sex and language, is for the monotheistic religions a fundamental axiom. Their destiny as religions, when they are true to it, makes them inevitably missionary. This presents one of the great dilemmas of history to which attention must later be drawn.

The *inclusive* intention

There is nothing simple about taking the Bible seriously. The exclusive demand is there, ultimately indispensable as an affirmation of the human mind, if the universe and man's experience are to make sense. No less clear is it that what is a demand upon faith is matched by an attitude which is as inclusive as the love of God. He makes his sun to rise on the evil as much as upon the good and the moral of that is that we are to reflect this all-embracing goodness of God (Matt. 5:45-48).

Scarcely has Jesus started his ministry before we find its all-embracing scope. In Mark 3:7-10 we see in anticipation a miniature of the great commission to 'all nations'. Again, there is that rare occasion during his earthly ministry when Jesus went into what was mainly Gentile territory (Mark 7:24-37). The time had not yet come for the wider working out of the commission, which explains the refusal of Jesus to exploit this opportunity. But there can be no doubt that in the mind of Jesus his message had a universal scope. How often he must have read the restrictive words which separated the court of the Gentiles from the more sacred area of the Temple, warning foreigners to go no further on pain of death. Was it this flagrant piece of religious exclusiveness which led him to quote one day from Isaiah 'My house shall be called a house of prayer for all the nations' (Mark 11:17)?

Consider again his attitude to those who were not Jews by faith. Of a Roman centurion's trust in him Jesus could say 'nowhere, even in Israel, have I found faith like this' (Luke 7:9). In the same Gospel there is a warning that, in the Last Day, heathen cities like Tyre and Sidon will have more hope of mercy than some cities of Israel (10:13-15). And this links up with that tremendous vision of the great assize in Matthew 25, where the final verdict will depend, not on orthodoxy of belief, but on practical loving kindness, a sobering reminder so rarely remembered.

The story of the Good Samaritan (Luke 10:29-37), and the promise of a future of illimitable possibility opened up to the Woman of Samaria (John 4:21-24), foretastes, both, of one of the first missionary enterprises of the apostolic Church; the expectation that the Kingdom would welcome people from the east and the west, the north and the south (Luke 13:29); the character of God as revealed in the parable of the father and his two sons (Luke 15:11-32); the wide-ranging insistence on the other sheep which are not of this particular fold (John 10:16); the very meaning of the Cross (John 12:32); the claim to be the Light of the World (John 8:12) — no responsible criticism queries that in all these passages we have an explicit recording of the inclusive intention of Jesus.

Clearly, long before the Gospels were written, those who understood the great commission had so interpreted it. Acts 1:8 is geographically inclusive and represents a commission which has never been cancelled or qualified and is still operative.

We have seen how Peter's encounter with a Roman centurion began to teach him and the other apostles that the gospel was for everyman. But it was Paul who most obviously led the Christian Church out into the wider world. A turning point for him, as we saw earlier, came at Pisidian Antioch. There, perhaps in a new way, he recognised fully that, in particular, it was to a mission to the Gentiles that he was commissioned. We have already seen in 1 Corinthians 9:19-23 (p.34) the way in which he put his obedience into action, surely one of the greatest definitions of the missionary method ever written. We see in Romans 2 the theology by which he supported such action. Deeper still was his awareness that the oneness of mankind was a oneness in mankind's slavery to sin (Rom. 3:23), only to be matched and surpassed by the oneness of God's liberating response through 'free grace alone' (3:24).

Paul drew far-reaching conclusions from this overwhelming sense of the unity of mankind. We find it in his understanding of the Adam in whom all men are one in their need of salvation, just as that salvation is to be found in the Christ who is Adam *redivivus* (Rom. 5:12-19, 1 Cor. 15:45-49). We find it in his speech to the pagans in Lystra, where he echoes the 'Sermon on the Mount' as showing us the generosity of God (Acts 14:15-17), later to follow this up in more sober mood in his letter to the Romans chapters 1 and 2. We find it again when, in Athens, he can happily quote a pagan poet Aratus, accepting that he had a genuine insight into the truth about God, an interesting anticipation of the second century Apologists and of Dante's appreciation of Virgil many centuries later. We see this sense of the unity that lies within creation and redemption in Romans chapters 9-11, which gives us Paul's interpretation of history; almost, indeed, the beginnings of a philosophy of Mission, with its dramatic conclusion of God's mercy to all mankind (11:32).

And even this does not exhaust Paul's thought. The passionate argument of Galatians, written early in his missionary career, pivots on chapter 3:28 — 'There is no such thing as Jew and Greek, slave and freeman, male and female; for you are all one person in Christ Jesus', an echo here of his use of the analogy of the two Adams. The word 'all' in Paul's vocabulary, in its embracing gravity and joyful anticipation, merits study as affording an insight into his warm-hearted personality, his fiery temperament, his enthusiasm for his calling, and his capacity for endurance.

But if ever a man had his eyes on the galaxies, in terms of the vast universe, then Paul had it. Paul, an heir of Greece no less than of Israel, was no stranger to the majesty of the natural world. Indeed, can we imagine such a man sleeping rough under the stars on countless journeys, watching them from the heaving planks of ships at sea, believing that all were the work of God, and not finding a place for this natural order in God's purpose of redemption? Only such a man could have described the created universe as itself looking forward to a fulfilment comparable to that prepared for mankind (Romans 8:19-25). Only such a man could write about Jesus that 'through him God chose to reconcile the whole universe to himself, making peace through the shedding of his blood upon the cross — to reconcile all things, whether on earth or in heaven, through him alone' (Col. 1:20).

What must we conclude from this double emphasis which runs right through the New Testament, as it is, also, one of the great themes of the Old Testament itself? The exclusive demand and the inclusive intention must be held together, however acute the tension. Each is inseparably part of the gospel. Trifle with either — and not to take both seriously is to trifle — is to abandon the proportion of the Faith, is to miss the challenge of the Great Commission. *The exclusive demand* is there to remind us of the gravity of choice, of the urgency present in all human affairs and in every human life, of our inescapable responsiblity to make it possible for all men to know what God has done, what God is doing, and what God will do. The *inclusive intention* gives to our obedience to the Great Commission an endurance based on hope (Rom. 5:4), a hope which Paul insists is 'no mockery because God's love has flooded our inmost heart through the Holy Spirit he has given us' (Romans 5:5).

At some place in Galilee, there came one of those post-Resurrection appearances of Jesus which were still a surprise and, as Matthew describes it, giving an authentic touch to the incident, some were in a maze, being 'doubtful'. It almost looks as if it was to the doubters that Jesus addressed himself:

> Jesus then came up and spoke to them. He said: "Full authority in heaven and on earth has been committed to me. Go forth therefore and make all nations my disciples; baptize men everywhere in the name of the Father and the Son and the Holy Spirit, and teach them to observe all that I have commanded you. And be assured that I am with you always, to the end of time" (Matt. 28:16-20).

Was this the same occasion described in the longer ending of Mark (16:14-18), in Luke 24:45-49, in John 21:1-13, and in Acts 1:3-11? Probably not. The disciples had always been extraordinarily obtuse in understanding Jesus, and tragically slow in their obedience, as Christians have been ever since. Almost certainly Jesus had to repeat himself again and again to get his meaning across, and these five passages represent a number of occasions in which it slowly dawned on those first disciples that, just as surely as Jesus himself had been sent as the Great Commission, so, in turn, he was sending them to the ends of the earth and to the end of time.

Part II will tell something of the bitter-sweet story of how the great commission was carried out in the next nineteen-hundred years.

PART II

The Church in History Spells it Out

We tell our Lord God plainly: If he will have his Church, then he must look how to maintain and defend it: for we can neither uphold nor protect it. And well for us, that it is so! For in case we could, or were able to defend it, we should become the proudest asses under heaven. Who is the Church's protector, that hath promised to be with her to the end, and the gates of hell shall not prevail against her? Kings, Diets, Parliaments, Lawyers? Marry, no such cattle.

Martin Luther
Table Talk

CHAPTER 1

The Commonplaces of Mission

AMONG MY MORE treasured possessions is a small faded pamphlet which I bought in 1924. I had just committed myself to what I hoped was to be a life-time's service as a missionary among the people of the household of Islam. The pamphlet had as its title *The Patience of God in Moslem Evangelisation.* The author was Dr. Samuel Zwemer who had already spent some years as a missionary in the Arabian peninsula. Not until thirty-nine years later did I have the privilege, while on one journey to the United States, of meeting Dr. Zwemer and thanking him for what that pamphlet had meant to me.

The patience of God — that surely is the only possible starting point for any theological understanding of the bitter-sweet story of how the Church in history has spelled-out and mis-spelled its great commission.

The whole Bible is one sustained commentary on the patience of God. How often in the Old Testament we can hear the throb in the heart of God as it has been relayed to us through the great prophets of Israel who had learnt to listen to him. And in the New Testament we watch with amazement and hope the patience of Jesus with his slow-witted disciples, and feel the amazement at his patience with us, and cherish the hope that in us too that patience may have some fruit.

That pamphlet of Dr. Zwemer's has stood me in good stead in my understanding of the Bible, in my own spiritual pilgrimage, and in my study of the history of the Church's missionary enterprise. I remain filled with amazement and with hope because of the continued patience of God.

The Gospel is Jesus

In Part I we have seen how clearly the writers of the New Testament recognised that the Great Commission is first of all the Person of Jesus himself, and only then an undertaking in which discipleship is involved. It would be fair to say that all through the long period of nineteen centuries with which Part II is concerned the emphasis on the Person of Jesus was never lost to sight, however variously it was interpreted. This element of fidelity is part of the 'sweetness' even when the record is most full of 'bitterness'. Paul, as a missionary, learnt this lesson the hard way. In his letter to the Christians in Galatia, we see how bitter a Christian missionary can be, how harshly he can contend for a truth which he believes is being betrayed. In 2 Corinthians 11:1-6 we find a rather gentler approach to a no less serious threat to what he so passionately believed about the gospel. Later still in what is the reflection of an old man near to death we see the supernatural triumph of 'sweetness' where 'bitterness' would have been so natural. In Philippians 1:15-18 'Some, indeed, proclaim Christ in a jealous and quarrelsome spirit; others proclaim him in true goodwill, and these are moved by love for me... But the others, moved by personal rivalry, present Christ from mixed motives, meaning to stir up fresh trouble for me as I lie in prison. What does it matter? One way or another, in pretence or in sincerity, Christ is set forth, and for that I rejoice.'

Yes, with whatever motives, and they have often been very mixed, Christ has been set forth. That is one fundamental continuity in the story of the Church's mission.

But there is also a genuine continuity in the underlying pattern by which the setting forth of Christ has been undertaken. We can trace this down the centuries expressed in four ways —

Preaching
Teaching
Healing
Witness

How variously these were interpreted we will see in the
following chapters. Here it will be enough to show in general
terms how we are to look for each of these threads in the whole
tapestry of events.

Preaching

The essential message of the preacher has always been the
Person of Jesus. The attention of unbelievers was drawn to
him. 'We come...as Christ's ambassadors' says Paul to the
Corinthians. The sense of being on an embassy, on a duty of
great dignity and great urgency is never lost. No less surely
were believers directed to Jesus as Saviour, as Lord, as Judge,
their lives being thus determined as to how to live. More has
been preserved of this element in Christian preaching than of
the preaching to unbelievers, in part for the very good reason,
consciously or unconsciously recognised, that conversion is not
something which can be inherited. For each individual, for
each generation it has to be experienced afresh, and always
there are new levels at which conversion has to be experienced.
It often takes quite a long time for conversion to reach the
cheque-book, or the wage-packet.

Preaching has, of course, taken more forms than exhortations
from the pulpit or in the market-place. It has often been done
by writing. As we shall see, apologists for the gospel have done
most of their preaching through books and pamphlets. Again,
there has been the way of controversy, of challenging what
is believed to be error by force of argument. And as important as any other way of preaching has been the translation
of the Bible into the languages of mankind, and its
world-wide distribution. In all these ways Jesus has been
preached.

It is also possible to discern in all ages a substantial unity in
the Message. There has been an insistence on the sovereignty
of God: there has been the offer of forgiveness and with that
the empowering for life by the Holy Spirit: there has been the
summons to faith and obedience.

Considering the record of Christian disunity it is one great
ground of hope that the unchanging gospel really has proved to
be unchanging, even when the terms in which it has been

translated have varied from culture to culture, from age to age.

Teaching

We too easily distinguish between preaching and teaching. Paul in the lecture-room of Tyrannus in Ephesus evangelised through teaching, almost certainly by what today we call 'dialogue' (Acts 19:9). Pantaenus, who may first have been a missionary to India, became head of the Catechetical School in Alexandria. He too was a teacher who evangelised through his teaching. Gregory Thaumaturgus, later to be bishop in his native Pontus, was converted by the quiet persistence and teaching of Origen. We make a great mistake if we overlook the converting ministry of theologians. Countless men and women have come to faith in Jesus because someone with a theologically trained mind was able to meet them at the point of their doubts and uncertainties.

And if conversion is to be in depth, then we can realise how important Paul saw it to be in that, immediately upon presenting the grandeur of the gospel, he should at once apply it to the practical affairs of everyday living. All of his epistles are full of just such applied gospel teaching. Christians, genuine believers, have to be reproved, rebuked, exhorted if they are to become indeed mature members of Christ's Body (Col. 1:28, 29). Paul was as strenuously occupied with this activity as he was in trying to reach those who were not Christians.

Healing

In Jesus we can distinguish three ways in which he saw the human situation. He saw that society itself was sick, and that this environment lay behind much of the sickness of individuals. This emerges clearly from a close study of Mark chapter 2, in which an apparently unrelated passage gives the key to the chapter. Verses 21-22 read, 'No-one sews a patch of unshrunk cloth on to an old coat; if he does, the patch tears away from it, the new from the old, and leaves a bigger hole. No-one puts new wine into old wine-skins; if he does, the wine will burst the skins, and then wine and skins are both lost.

Fresh skins for new wine!' Innumerable other illustrations of this very inconvenient challenge of Jesus can be found in the Gospels.

He saw human need at every level and his compassion moved him to action. His text for his first sermon in Nazareth (Luke 4:18-19), quoted from Isaiah 61, sets the pattern of his healing ministry.

And it is clear from many an incident that he was not satisfied with any healing which did not make a man 'every whit whole'. He knew that sin was as much a cause of illness as any virus or infection — sin corporate and sin individual. In Mark 6:12-13, the account of the first mission of the disciples, we find them preaching repentance and dealing with sickness. In Luke 10:9 the heralding of a new order goes side by side with healing the sick when Jesus sends out the seventy disciples on a second mission.

The significance of those two early missionary journeys has never quite been lost. However little understanding men might have of the causes of disease, however superstitious they might become about ways of healing, the tradition of compassion for human suffering has moved Christians to action. A literal translation of the last will and testament of Francis of Assisi opens with these words —

See in what manner God gave it to me, to me, Brother Francis, to begin to do penitence; when I lived in sin, it was very painful to me to see lepers, but God himself led me into their midst, and I remained here a little while. When I left them, that which had seemed to me bitter had become sweet and easy.

That is authentic New Testament. There have never been lacking some with the same compassion. Long before Francis kissed a leper Christians had been founding hospitals. In the century before Francis, the Knights of the Order of St. John of Jerusalem had added the care of the sick to their provision of help for pilgrims. With the advance of medical science medical work became a regular feature of missionary pioneering.

Nevertheless it has to be admitted that during the centuries since the New Testament there has been an ambiguous element in the record of Christian healing. Because, for many centuries, there was universal ignorance of the nature of disease, healings became invested with an aura of the miraculous. In the Middle Ages this frequently led to mass hysteria, itself often shamelessly exploited by interested parties, not a few clergy amongst them. Exorcism, from being intimately related to the gospel, to penitence and to prayer, gradually tended to become a ritual, not always easily distinguishable by the observer from magic and witchcraft which have always haunted the recesses of the human mind, and still do.

That the prayer of faith can heal the sick has never been doubted. There are many Christians today for whom healing is seen as being an essential part of the charismatic ministry of the Church. Among the Independent Churches in Africa healing by prayer and the laying on of hands is a primary activity of the Church's ministry.

But an uneasy ambiguity remains. The gulf between the practice of scientific medicine and what is called spiritual healing is still, for all practical purposes, unbridged. The materialist philosophy which underlies much medical practice maintains the gulf. But it is also true that on the part of Christians there has been far too little grateful acceptance of the fact that all knowledge comes from God and that, in the field of healing, modern surgery, medicine, and psychiatry are also channels of God's grace. Because Christians have been so tardy in giving this recognition it is hardly surprising that their co-operation *qua* Christians is so rarely invited t y the medical profession.

What is at least possible is that in our very sick modern society, viewed nationally and internationally, the Christian Church may yet come into its own as healer and reconciler. This is still only a possibility because the world can fairly say to a divided Church 'Physician heal thyself'. Yet the possibility is there. And if our interpretation of the evidence of the Gospels is correct, then in this, as in every other respect, we need to look at the sickness of our society and at all illness through the eyes of Jesus. There is one New Testament word, *agape,* which cannot be translated into any language. It can only be translated into action. Jesus said to his friends 'as I have loved you, so you are to love one another. If there is this love *(agape)*

among you, then all will know that you are my disciples' (John
13:35). Nineteen hundred years have passed and we have still
not learnt that art of translating the untranslatable into action.
The patience of God, how we try it!

Witness

This was something at once individual and corporate and the
two are best not disentangled, for the very heart of Christianity
lies in the description of the Church as the 'Body of Christ' and
the individual Christian as a member of the Body (1 Cor.
12:27). That remembered, there is, running like a golden
thread through all the vicissitudes of history, the witness given
by the individual Christian both by lip and life. There seem to
have been from the earliest times four ways in which
Christians spoke of their Faith. They gossiped it: they
defended it: they bore testimony: they witnessed by life as well
as by lip.

'Gossip' is a word which has become debased coinage. But
in its earliest usage it referred to God, god-parents being
relations 'in God'. But if we think of it as informal conversation, as 'chattering', we can get a homely understanding of how
individuals spread the Faith. Those ordinary simple Christians
who were scattered after the death of Stephen were certainly
not all preachers in any accepted sense of the word. They *told*
about Jesus (Acts 8:4). Shakespeare in *Twelfth Night* makes
Viola describe how if she were Olivia she would for love's sake
'make the babbling gossip of the air cry out "Olivia"'. That is a
worthy use of our word, gossip. So we must picture many an
individual Christian making his 'babbling gossip' cry out
"Jesus". This is how we are to understand Paul's urging of the
Christians in Colossae — 'Behave wisely to those outside your
own number; use the present opportunity to the full. Let
your conversation be always gracious, and never insipid;
study how best to talk with each person you meet' (Col.
4:5-6). Behind those words about using the present opportunity
there is, in the Greek, the picture of the market-place where
bargains are bought up. But even more is implied in
the New Testament use which carries with it the idea of
actually redeeming, ransoming, paying a price for, taking

the opportunity. Gossiping the Gospel, God-spel, may lead to unexpected consequences. There is always some danger in the air where witness is concerned.

But the analogy of the market-place remains true to life. I well remember attending a service of Holy Communion in a remote part of Nigeria. It was a great gathering of over six hundred communicants. After the service I asked how the gospel had reached this area, and I was told that it was due to two market-women who gossiped to such good effect that many became curious and asked for someone to teach them about this 'new way'. An African catechist was sent. To a far greater extent than is commonly realised Africa has been evangelised by gossiping the gospel.

In the early nineteenth century, William Wilberforce, one of society's 'darlings', found his 'market-place' in fashionable social gatherings. He took Paul's advice with great seriousness. Studying how best to talk, he prepared what he called 'launchers' — phrases, remarks, calculated to turn a conversation in a serious direction. Such a man could have proved a prig and a bore but, writes a contemporary, 'when the little man came in late to a dinner party, bristling maybe with "launchers", every face lighted up with pleasure at his entry'. He took Paul's counsel to heart and his conversation was always gracious.

We could well seek to redeem the meaning of 'gossip'. It has proved one of the great methods of Christian witness.

As we shall see in the next chapter, the Christian man or woman might at any moment be called upon to make his defence. 1 Peter 3:15 bids the Christian 'be always ready with your defence'. And in that context he tells them not to be afraid but 'hold the Lord Christ in reverence in your hearts'. This surely is a reference back to the warning of Jesus that persecution lay ahead and that this would be an 'opportunity to testify' (Luke 21:12-13).

Making a 'defence' may involve no more than giving a reason for your faith, speaking from experience, something which might well happen in the course of conversation with friends. But it also carried with it the meaning of bearing witness in a law court when, in answer to an accusation, you had to testify.

Christians down the centuries have known how to bear witness by lip, however inarticulate they may have been.

But they had another witness to give and always have had. 'Love must not be a matter of words or talk; it must be genuine, and show itself in action. This is how we may know that we belong to the realm of truth...' (1 John 3:18-19). Love, joy, peace — these were the cardinal virtues for which the Christian was empowered by the Holy Spirit (Gal. 5:22). And it is clear from the New Testament that these words are meant to be infectious. They are essentially contagious, the germs of health, the real anti-bodies to the germs of disease which Paul has so accurately diagnosed in the previous verses (Gal. 5:19-21). But to change the metaphor, we ought to be clear that if there are fruits of the Spirit in our lives they are there for others to pick. No Christian can live for himself alone. The fruits of the Spirit are common property.

The Christian's witness by life was the very ground of his witness by lip. The New Testament is crystal clear that for the believer there is a standard of reference for all his living which admits of no compromise. He is a 'Christ-bearer'. Paul dramatically expresses this in his treatment of illicit sex in 1 Corinthians 6:12-20. But, in fact, his insistence on the oneness of the Christian with Christ is the basic theme of every one of his letters. It is dangerous to speak of the Church as the 'extension of the Incarnation', attractive as the phrase is: and it has a proper meaning. But the Church, as we know it in history, has far too often been apostate, and has by its complacency and by its complicity with the world, effectively denied Christ. We are on far surer ground if we content ourselves with the Pauline metaphor of the 'Body of Christ' which, as in a great mystery, and in ways far beyond our understanding, is the abiding reality of the Great Commission himself, of whom, by faith-obedience, we become a part.

If I have first stressed the witness of the individual it has been of set purpose. The Christian Faith has spread throughout the world, in the main, through the witness of men and women whose names are known only to God. They are an anonymous company as far as the records of history go. There is, however, another sense in which the word 'anonymous' can be used. It can be used to describe those who do certainly believe in Jesus

Christ as both Saviour and Lord but who for various reasons, some very understandable, will not confess his name and will not accept membership in any Christian community. They prefer to remain un-named, anonymous. Later we shall want to understand the argument of those who appear to approve anonymity. Yet, a distinction does exist between the nameless, because unknown, and the deliberately anonymous. And this distinction needs to be maintained. There is an inescapable sense in which the experience of salvation is related to open confession (Romans 10:9). We serve no good purpose by clouding the issue.

Witnessing Together

Behind the individual, however, and implicit in the phrase, the Body of Christ, lies the corporate witness of Christians in their conscious communion with one another 'in Christ'. The first eight verses of almost the shortest book of the Bible, 3 John, give a beautiful picture of a Christian home. Was the Gaius there addressed the same as the one Paul saluted as 'Gaius my host and host of the whole congregation' (Rom. 16:23)? We cannot be certain. Gaius was a very common name. But the portraits of both men have a common likeness. Here we see the house-church, the earliest corporate expression of Christian fellowship. There is ample New Testament evidence that it was such Christian homes which were the centres of corporate witness. It was in such homes that Christians worshipped together, and from which they went out to put love into practice, centuries before there were any church buildings. This may yet become the common pattern once again. It is already the only pattern in China as these words are being written.

And it was in such homes that Christians first demonstrated the revolutionary ethics that they were introducing to the world. We read Colossians 3:12-4:1 so easily. We miss the fact that it was social and political dynamite and that, as its implications were worked out, they turned the world upside down. Here, in relations between husband and wife, we have for the first time an ethic of mutual and reciprocal obligation. Again, in the ancient world a child had no rights against his parents. He was not a person in his own right. Here we find a new relationship being established. Most of all this was true of the relation of master and slave. In the world into which the gospel first went out the slave was a thing. He or she was not a person, but quite literally a chattel. No doubt many a slave was well-treated. Many slaves were able to purchase their freedom. Some came to occupy high positions of responsibility. But these were the exceptions.

Something new was being created in households like those of Gaius, Narcissus, Philemon and many others. And, throughout succeeding centuries, Christian homes have sweetened life in every country in the world. Today they are perhaps the most effective means of grace that God is using in a society which is disintegrating, as it reverts to the conditions of an older, more brutal world. It is part of the bitterness of the record that, in so many ways, Christians, as individuals, and the Christian Church as a community, have failed, and still fail to measure up to anywhere near the standard set by the New Testament. How very patient is God!

The Church in history

Before following the story from the first century to the twentieth a word is needed to explain the titles of the following chapters.

Church history as a descriptive term is a dangerous misnomer. Strictly speaking there is no such thing as Church history. What we can recognise, and must try to recognise more fully, is that the Church is *in* history. Of course it has another dimension. It is *in* Christ. It can never be confined within the limitations of history. Its life at the profoundest level 'lies hidden with Christ in God' (Col. 3:3). Yet it remains true that there is a Church which is *in via*. It is a pilgrim Church and its journey takes it through what we call history. Just as surely as Christian in Bunyan's tale rarely, if ever, found himself alone, and was for ever meeting with other men, was influenced by them, and often came to much mischief by losing his sense of direction, so it has been with the Christian Church.

We will be wise then, while ever keeping in mind that other

dimension, to take all history seriously. This, after all, is involved if we take the Incarnation of our Lord seriously. Jesus of Nazareth was an historical person. It was one of the deadliest of all heresies to claim that he was not truly man (1 John 4:1-4).

The writer of that Epistle had no doubt about it, to deny the reality of the Incarnation was to be 'Antichrist'. Isolating the Church from history is another way of being anti-Christ. For this reason I have given the following chapters titles which explicitly relate the Church to the general history of mankind.

Chapter 2 — From the sack of Jerusalem by Titus to the
         sack of Rome by Alaric the Goth
         A.D. 70 — A.D. 410

Chapter 3 — From the battle of Badr to the capture of
         Constantinople by the Turks
         A.D. 624 — A.D. 1453

Chapter 4 — From the little ships of Diaz, Columbus and da
         Gama to the sinking of the Russian fleet by
         the Japanese in the straits of Tsushima
         A.D. 1492 — A.D. 1905

Chapter 5 — From man in the air to man on the moon
         July 25, 1909 — July 20, 1969

The chapter titles betray the standpoint of a man of the West. Yet it is true to history that Western man only very slowly became aware of the wider world of humankind. And Christianity, for all that it was born in Asia, gravitated westwards into the Graeco-Roman world. This, as we shall see, had far-reaching consequences for the Christian Faith. The genuine discovery of the rest of mankind by the man of the West is a contemporary experience. Obviously, then, very great humility is called for in interpreting history. There is so much we do not know and cannot know of the thoughts and actions of men in the past, even of our own western past which is reasonably well documented. The twentieth century has been described as the century of the common man. But the common man is the real subject of all history. He is the constant factor. This may be one reason why the Saviour of the common man simply called himself the Son of Man. He was born in the stable of a common inn. He worked as a common carpenter. He chose very common companions. His first missionaries were described as 'uneducated, common men' (Acts 4:13 R.S.V.). This is a continuing feature of the story.

CHAPTER 2

From the Sack of Jerusalem by Titus to the Sack of Rome by Alaric the Goth A.D. 70 - A.D. 410

WE, WHO IN our own day have watched Independence Movements pass from resentment at the indignity of being a subject people to flaming revolt against alien rule, ought to have a lively understanding of the social and political background of the New Testament. Too easily we read the Gospels and the Epistles out of context. Palestine under Roman rule, in addition to economic distress, was seething with discontent. How many must have used Psalm 123 as an almost daily prayer, 'Have mercy upon us, O Lord, have mercy upon us, for we have had more than enough of contempt. Too long our soul has been sated with the scorn of those who are at ease, the contempt of the proud' (R.S.V.).

We know that there was widespread expectancy that God was going to intervene. There was that highly significant moment when Jesus realised that a popular movement wanted to proclaim him as its revolutionary leader (John 6:15). At another level there are those revealing sentences in John's Gospel (11:45-53), where the real trial of Jesus took place in his absence. Put ourselves in the situation of the Members of the Council, hating Roman rule, acutely aware of national discontent, and yet no less acutely aware that a premature revolt would lead to national disaster — and no doubt, as an important factor, the loss of their own position of privilege.

We are likely to arrive at a far deeper understanding of the mood in much of Asia and Africa and Latin America in this second half of the twentieth century if we try to enter with real understanding into the temper of the Jewish people in Palestine in the first half of the first century. Jesus understood it. Can we doubt that he had a deep sympathy with his people? That he should have deliberately chosen, as two of his inner circle the freedom-fighters Simon the Zealot and Judas Iscariot is some measure of his understanding. That he died for refusing to satisfy the dreams of his people is not the whole of the meaning of his death nor the whole of the reason for it. But his refusal of the way of violence was certainly one reason for his own violent death.

With all this in mind we approach the moment when the longing for freedom from foreign rule could not be restrained. In A.D. 66 open rebellion began and it took four years of desperate fighting before the trained soldiery of Rome finally overcame the fanatical courage of the rebels and Jerusalem was sacked, the rebellion ending in A.D. 73 with the epic story of Masada.

There was to be a final flare-up in A.D. 132 when Bar Kochba led another rebellion. But the sack of Jerusalem by Titus is the really decisive date, in more ways than one, in the bitter-sweet story of how the Church went out into the world with its commission.

Christians and Jews

A.D. 70 sees the real break in relationship between Christians and Jews. Consider the reaction of the Jews, proud of their heritage, jealous for their faith, holding fast to the tradition of their fathers. It must have been gall and bitterness to them when sometime, between A.D. 66 and A.D. 70, the Christians left Jerusalem to its fate and found safety in Pella on the other side of Jordan. There had still been up till then a great many Christians of Jewish background who sought to hold their new-found convictions about Jesus while maintaining an observance of Jewish law and custom. The evacuation to Pella and the sack of Jerusalem brought that experiment to an end.

But if we are to understand the growing bitterness of Jewry against the Christians, we must try to see what it must have felt like in A.D. 70 and its tragic aftermath for a Jew to see what Christians were doing with the Jewish heritage. The great German historian, Harnack, was not exaggerating when he wrote of the Gentile Church 'stripping Judaism of everything'.

The Jewish scriptures were appropriated and given an interpretation no Jew could accept. The Christians claimed to be
the 'true Israel' and that the Jews were apostate. The Torah,
round which Jews rallied after their Babylonian captivity, and
more than ever after A.D. 70, was dismissed as being overtaken
by the new law of Christ. And their expected redeemer was
identified with one who was hanged on a tree, the 'cursed of
God', of whom the unknown author of the *Teaching of the
Apostles*, written about the year A.D. 100, could write of being
'saved by the Curse Himself.' What, indeed, would a devout
Jew have made of Paul's argument in Galatians 3:10-14? If a
Jewish victim of the sack of Jerusalem ended as a slave in
Rome there must have been a grim irony, supposing he ever
read Paul's letter to the Galatians, to read Ch. 4: 21-31. Verse
25 would have a poignancy we can hardly feel, as such a Jewish
slave read 'Jerusalem of today, for she and her children are in
slavery'. Harnack was not exaggerating when he went on to say
that the Gentile Church 'cut off all connections with the parent
religion. The daughter first robbed her mother and then
repudiated her'.

This is an unfamiliar way of looking at the story of the
spread of the Gospel. But perhaps it is a salutary one. It does at
least help to explain the tremendous bitterness which, until
very recent times, Jews have felt for Christians. It explains
why the 13th Benediction of the Jewish liturgy was prefaced by
so terrible a denunciation of slanderers, informers and traitors,
which must, understandably, have had special reference to
Christians.

And this bitterness was sadly matched by the Christians.
Bishop Lightfoot in his book *The Apostolic Fathers* gives it as
his considered judgment that the book known as *The Epistle of
Barnabas* was written between A.D. 70 and A.D. 79. We, as
Christians, can rejoice in that author's claim that 'the Kingdom
of Jesus is on the cross', and see the whole book as an
interpretation of what the cross of Calvary really means. Yet at
the same time it is a devastating critique of Judaism and of the
Jews' own interpretation of their own Scriptures.

What, alas, is quite certain is that, with the Apologists of the
second century, the total break with Judaism is a constant
theme, often handled with arrogance, Justin Martyr's *Dialogue*

with Trypho being in a measure a happy exception. By the second century we have moved a long way from a Jesus who could weep over Jerusalem, from a Paul who could 'even pray to be outcast from Christ myself for the sake of my brothers, my natural kinsfolk. They are Israelites: they were made God's sons; theirs is the splendour of the divine presence, theirs the covenants, the law, the temple worship, and the promises. Theirs are the patriarchs, and from them, in natural descent, sprang the Messiah. May God, supreme above all, be blessed for ever! Amen.' (Rom. 9:3-5).

I have thus dwelt on the significance of A.D. 70 and its sequel because it represents the first dramatic failure of the Church to be true to its commission. And that failure has continued down history as regards the Jewish people. There is a terrible Christian responsibility for centuries of persecution of the Jews, for the very conception of a ghetto, for the pogroms in so many professedly Christian countries. With that record, dare we plead 'not guilty' when we contemplate Auschwitz and Belsen?

Thank God this is not the whole story. Thank God that in our own day some tentative steps are being taken to recognise the 'Christian' root of anti-Semitism. But the sordid story needs to be remembered. Because it is so uncomfortable it is too easily forgotten.

In writing of the tragic failure of the Christian Church to bear a Christ-like witness to the Jews I am not calling in question the uniqueness of God's revelation in Jesus. Witness to this uniqueness is the point of standing or falling of the Church. I am sure that, in the light of this uniqueness, the Christian must have a distinctive interpretation of God's acts in history and therefore a particular understanding of God's revelation of himself through the Old Testament and the history of Israel therein recorded. In starting this chapter as I have, it is in part to insist that the validity of our claim to have a gospel for the world depends in part upon the integrity with which we are prepared to face our failures. We will have plenty of cause to need such integrity in the rest of Part II. Suffice it here to say that, had Christians made their witness to the Jews with a fraction of the grace and patience and courage and wisdom with which they made it to the Gentiles, history

would have been very different. To that witness to the Gentiles
we now turn.

The challenge to the Gentile world

Such records as we possess of Christian writings in the early
centuries, and they increase rapidly in number after the second
century, have one clear and distinctive theme. It is the theme,
'Jesus is Lord.' And, Christians were bold in proclaiming him
as such. There is interesting testimony in the *First Apology* of
Justin, addressed to the Emperor Antoninus Pius (c. A.D. 150),
that the Christians of his day looked back in wonder at the
obedience of the first Apostles to their commission. He writes
— 'From Jerusalem there did go out men, twelve in number,
into the world, and these, unlearned and with no ability in
speech, and in the power of God, they proclaimed (Christ) to
every race of men.' Again, in his *Dialogue with Trypho,*
addressed to the Jews, he can use an analogy they would
appreciate — 'The Twelve Apostles depend on the power of
God, as the twelve bells hung on the High Priest's robe, and
through their voice it is that all the earth has been filled with
the glory and the grace of God and of his Christ.'

The Church of the second and third centuries trod in the
steps of the Apostles. If one wishes to find later evidence of
that 'boldness' which characterised Peter and John before the
rulers and elders and doctors of the law, not to mention the
High Priestly family, as reported in Acts 4:5-13, it is only
necessary to read the seven letters of Ignatius, the belligerent
bishop of Antioch. Written on his way to martyrdom, they
reveal incredible vigour and utter fearlessness. They are deeply
Christ-centred. Christ crucified and risen is his theme. In his
letter to the Church in Smyrna he has a fine sentence about
bringing to repentance men who were compromising the faith,
seeking for them to 'return to the passion which is our
resurrection'. For Ignatius, as for Paul, the passion and
resurrection of Jesus is something in which the Christian
shares, not only by his faith but by his own living and dying.

How far the writings of the second and third century
apologists were read by others than Christians we have no
means of knowing. They were certainly directed to others. One

of the most moving is that addressed by an unknown writer around A.D. 140 to a man called Diognetus, quite possibly the tutor of the Emperor Marcus Aurelius. The writer believes that Diognetus is genuine in his desire to know more about the Christian Faith. First, the author deals with polytheism with something of the sarcasm of the prophet Isaiah. Then he distinguishes Christianity from Judaism. Only then does he make a magnificent statement about Jesus, which echoes the Prologue of John's Gospel, and Paul's argument in Chapters 1 and 2 of Colossians. There is something quite breathtaking in the boldness of his claims for Jesus. What the writer to the Hebrews says of Jesus as 'the effulgence of God's splendour and the stamp of God's very being', who 'sustains the universe by his word of power' (1:3) is here expanded with lyrical enthusiasm. There was nothing shy about the early Apologists, and they made their claims without any hesitation about one who had been crucified under Pontius Pilate. This might be 'a stumbling-block to Jews and folly to Greeks', but they were proving over the years that Jesus is 'the power of God and the wisdom of God' (1 Cor. 1:24). This witness is as valid today as when Diognetus read it and was, no doubt, greatly astonished, as were the other recipients of these remarkable tracts for the times.

But these early writings, good evidence as they are for the way in which the Christians pressed their case, making their defence, and giving a reason for the hope that was in them, reached only a very limited public. Probably, as has been suggested earlier, gossiping the gospel was the way in which the Faith was most effectively communicated. The House Churches in the early centuries, and their successors today, were the natural centres in which a new enthusiasm could be transmitted.

To the 'Regions beyond'

Paul's mobile ministry, his aim always to move on to new places, his desire to preach the gospel where it had not yet been heard, set a pattern which has never been lost. Whatever the precise function of the 'prophets' as designated in Paul's list of charismatic gifts for the upbuilding of the Church, however they were distinguished from the evangelists, it is clear that by the date of the *Didache*, the prophets were exercising an itinerant ministry. The *Didache* is concerned to guard against the abuse of this ministry and clearly it was sometimes abused. Drifting from place to place and trading on the hospitality of the local Christian congregations was a temptation for some. The *Didache* is draconian in its standard of treatment not least if the 'prophets' ask for money. There is a nice test — 'Not every one that speaks in the Spirit is a prophet, only if he has the manners of the Lord.' Yet, nevertheless theirs was an important ministry. Not elected by the churches they responded to what they felt was a call from God. Their lives, the message they proclaimed, and the spiritual fruits of their preaching were their credentials.

These wandering preachers set a pattern which is with us till this day. It was just such men of restless energy, the monks of Ireland, who played so considerable a part in evangelising the barbarian invaders of the Roman Empire. Then in the Middle Ages came the Friars. The Lollards in England and Huss in Bohemia were the forerunners of countless travelling preachers at the time of the Reformation. Parallel in devotion were men like Francis Xavier in his adventurous missionary journeys, and the Jesuits of Upper Canada who, in such numbers, died as victims of savagery, but proved to be the seed of the Church. And in Britain there were men as varied as George Fox and, most notable of all, John Wesley, not forgetting their continental peers the Moravians. Just such wanderers in our own century have been a host of African evangelists, Indians, Koreans, Chinese, and South Sea Islanders.

'Open-air' preaching was not confined to roving preachers. Bishops like Gregory in Pontus, or Irenaeus in Gaul, or Cyprian of Carthage were, for all their settled responsibilities, as active in evangelism. They were typical, not exceptional.

When, in due course, the ages of persecution by pagan emperors ended and toleration of a kind was the rule, there came another great age of preaching, more settled in character but no less evangelistic. Chrysostom of Antioch was as fearless a preacher of righteousness as Ignatius had been in a more precarious age, though not a more precarious episcopate. Chrysostom, by virtue of the pulpit he occupied, is in some ways the prototype of the great settled preaching ministries which have played so signal a part in the Church's obedience to its commission — he and his contemporaries, Ambrose of Milan and Augustine of Hippo. No century has lacked such men, though not all have been as golden-tongued as Chrysostom.

There will, however, be a significant lack in our understanding of the achievement of this preaching ministry, peripatetic or settled, if we fail to grasp the magnitude of the task which confronted men who sought to interpret a Faith, first formulated in a Hebrew setting, in categories which would convince the Hellenistic world. We see in the New Testament the interpretative skill of Paul and John, as in their several ways, they spoke into that world of thought so alien to the Hebrew tradition. Certainly Paul's letters demonstrate how much time he had to spend in correcting misunderstandings of what he meant. Jewish hearers understood him well enough, and often fiercely disagreed with him. It was the Gentiles who misinterpreted him. Again, in the Johannine Epistles, there is evidence of how difficult it could be to accept the full meaning of the Incarnation and its implications for life. In the letters to the Seven Churches in the Book of the Revelation it is plain to see how hard it was to convince Gentile Christians that the freedom with which Christ set men free was freedom, not licence.

With the second century came the great educational task of the Apologists, among whom were men like Clement of Alexandria and in the next century Origen. They, and others like them, used the subtleties of Greek thought to convey the gospel. In the process they compelled the Church to think through the meaning of its experience, giving to that experience a coherent form and a philosophy. This was a vast and comprehensive task, necessary if the mind of man was to be enlisted in the task of 'thinking God's thoughts after him', which was to be the responsibility of later centuries. It is no accident that modern scientific thought has been cradled in that Greek thinking which had received the profound impress of the Judaeo-Christian affirmation about the unity of the created universe, an ordered complexity under the directing control of the One God. It was the monotheism of the great prophets of Israel and of the great Greek theologians of the early Christian centuries which combined to create a frame for human thought which, in turn, made possible the spectacular achievements of modern science.

But for this achievement a considerable price had to be paid. The argumentative genius of the Greek mind which has yielded such a unique contribution to mankind's development, had the side effect of encouraging argument for argument's sake. And once it was accepted that truth could be encapsulated in propositions, there followed the *damnosa hereditas* of religious controversy. There is nothing wrong with controversy in itself. It becomes damnable only when truths about the Truth completely obscure him who is the Truth. That this has been a commonplace in the history of the Church is part of the bitterness, a very large part of the bitterness, of its story, and one major reason why it has failed to demonstrate a unity capable of dealing with the disunities of mankind.

Translating the gospel

Interpreting the gospel into new thought forms today will confront us as a major subject in Part III. The early centuries have much to teach us about how easy it is to become so preoccupied with language and terminology that we lose sight of the fact that man is much more than his mind, and that the gospel is concerned with the whole man, a person who can be loved, but very rarely argued, into faith.

One way of interpreting the gospel has from the earliest days involved the translation of the Bible from the original vernaculars of Hebrew and Greek. Two of the most influential translations ever made were those by St. Jerome and Ulphilas. St. Jerome completed the translation of the Bible into Latin in 404. Ulphilas translated the Bible into Gothic a few years earlier. Known as the Vulgate, St. Jerome's translation was the standard version for more than a thousand years and shaped the Christianity of Western Europe. Ulphilas, in translating the Bible, began the conversion of the barbarians who were to be the invaders and conquerors of the Roman Empire. One of those barbarians, Alaric, who sacked Rome, may not have been an ornament of the Christian Faith but he was enough of a

Christian to insist on the Church buildings in Rome being treated as sanctuaries into which men, women and children could be shepherded before the horrors of the sacking of the city. By these two translations it can be reasonably claimed that a large part of the missionary work of the Church in the Dark Ages was made possible and the Church of the West enabled to survive.

Max Müller, the great nineteenth century expert on the study of language, has this comment on the word 'barbarian', which was the contemptuous term used by Greeks of those who spoke other languages.

> Not till that word *barbarian* was struck out of the dictionary of mankind, and replaced by *brother,* not till the right of all nations of the world to be classed as one genus or kind was recognised, can we look even for this first beginnings of our science of language... This change was effected by Christianity.

The wholeness of salvation

Meanwhile another very effective form of witness was being continued, deliberately inspired by the Great Commission himself — the ministry of healing. We, in the second half of the twentieth century, are living in a time of universal upheaval, a time in which a revolution of rising expectations is finding almost universal frustration: when violence is the easiest response to frustration: when a sense of purposelessness is a pervasive atmosphere: a world in which the temperature of Faith is cool. We should without too much difficulty be able to imagine the very similar world of the centuries we are considering, with this added dimension of a vast ignorance of the causes of disease, and as a result the imputation of every distemper of the mind as well as the body to demonic forces.

First and foremost, the Christian witness was that all the forces of evil had been conquered by Christ's death on the Cross: they might be as malignant as ever but they were powerless when confronted in his Name. And his Name was no mere incantation or magic spell. Its moral power resided in the serenity of the Christian, himself or herself, being without fear, and therefore able to use the Name as an assurance born of experience. Exorcism, in these centuries, was one very real form by which the Gospel of Christ's victory was communicated. Prayers and the recitation of the Creed, besides the laying on of hands, were integral to this form of therapy.

But always there was something else which lay behind the man or woman, priest or layman, who practised what came for a time to be a specialist ministry in the Church — that of the exorcist. This was the compassion of the Christian community. This must not be underestimated. With almost pathetic slowness modern medical science is beginning to realise the place of the community in the healing of minds and bodies. The Church of the early centuries knew that there was a healing power in love which could work miracles. One illustration must suffice. In A.D. 252 an appalling visitation of plague struck Carthage. It was to rage over the whole Mediterranean world. Two emperors died of it. In the great city of Alexandria, within four years the population was reduced by half. Christians responded with such reckless courage in Alexandria that, at the cost of countless lives, they rallied pagans to help in what has been described as an 'excess of tenderness, such as scarcely could be justified except by the moral effect of intrepidity upon a population'. In Carthage, where as in Alexandria, the Christian bishop was a leading citizen, Cyprian proposed and carried out a scheme for the systematic care of the city. We read of how under the spur of his personal influence, following a great sermon on 'their Christian belief in their veritable Sonship to God', rich and poor alike responded to his challenge. And, so we are told, 'formed an adequate staff for the nursing and burial of sufferers and victims, without any discrimination of religious profession'. Archbishop Benson in his *Cyprian — his Life, his Times, his Work*, from which I have quoted, ends these particular references with the sentence, 'that effort to grapple with a Plague-city must have been as energetic as it was novel'.

That devastating plague coincided with one of the great persecutions of the Christians. Terror-stricken pagans called on their gods for protection and, as is common in times of panic, looked for scapegoats. There were plenty available who refused any worship to the gods, or even to the emperor.

Cyprian and the Christians were being persecuted even while they saved Carthage. The Christians who died from nursing the victims of plague were no less martyrs than those who died in the arena in Rome or were executed or burnt alive in provincial cities throughout the world. Witness can take many forms. If more is not written here of the martyrs of these early centuries it is in part because they should not be distinguished from the multitude of their successors, whose own self-sacrifice has been a continuing ministry of healing and reconciliation in the chronically diseased body of mankind.

Can 'Caesar' be Christian?

Two and a half centuries of endurance of intermittent persecution, and continual suspicion of the Christians as enemies of the State, came to a breath-taking climax when Constantine, perhaps for reasons of State, perhaps from conviction, but probably from a little of both, decided to become a Christian.

This event provoked the dramatic question to which no wholly satisfactory answer has ever been given — what happens when Caesar wants to become a Christian? Or, to put it another way — in what sense can a state be called Christian? It is easy to understand the enormous sense of relief felt by Christians in the year 313 when the Edict of Toleration was issued. For them, at least, there was *now* no difficulty about the interpretation of Romans 13:1-8 and 1 Peter 2:13-17. Much more difficult was the question of how to apply the words of Jesus in relation to Tiberius — 'Pay Caesar what is due to Caesar, and pay God what is due to God' (Mark 12:17). That question haunts us still. For much more than a thousand years the ideal of a 'godly prince' held society in some measure of cohesion wherever there was a Christian community. But very early we have a shrewd comment by St. Augustine of Hippo — 'It would really be more fitting to speak of good Christians as kings, than to call bad princes so. The former in seeking the glory of God rule themselves. The latter seeking their own lusts are enemies to themselves and tyrants to others. The former are the body of that true king, Christ; the latter are the body of their father the devil'. That was written in his *De*

Doctrina Christiana somewhere around A.D. 400. That is a piece of remarkable foresight written within a few years of the death of Theodosius, the emperor during whose reign occurred the first great mass-movement into the Christian Church.

At this point it is important for our subject to realise that when the Empire became 'officially' Christian a wholly new situation confronted those concerned with carrying out the great commission. They had few precedents to guide them.

Caesar himself presented a tremendous problem. Constantine naturally assumed that he must play an important part in the affairs of the Church. The Council of Nicea of A.D. 325 was of his contriving and proceeded under his presidency. Very naturally he saw the Church as the ideal cement of his empire, as did his successors. The bishops appreciated this role for the Church, but were already preoccupied with the question of the Church's own unity. And that unity was to prove hard to come by, once it was accepted as axiomatic that unity meant uniformity of belief, expressed in propositions, and uniformity of order expressed in terms of hierarchy and precedence. We are still wrestling with these problems in the twentieth century, with Caesar now manifested under very different guise from a Constantine or a Theodosius.

Mass movements pose problems

Again, the New Testament had little guidance to give to a Church confronted with a vast influx of pagans whose Christian convictions and understanding were strictly limited. In the Churches to which Paul addressed his letters there were plenty of contentious Christians and, no doubt, many who were 'babes in the Faith'. Yet for them, as for the Christians of the next 250 years, it was as dangerous as it was difficult to be a Christian. But now, baptism had become little more significant of faith than had been the pagan's offering of a pinch of incense to the genius of the Emperor.

And pagans brought their pagan morals into the Church. That is why so much Christian preaching became preoccupied with moral exhortation, and continued so for many centuries as hordes of pagans continued to press into the Church.

We may note two responses to this unprecedented situation, a movement and a book.

A movement that shaped history

Revulsion against the erosion of Christian moral standards, and also resentment against increasing regimentation by the now 'Christian' state, acting as censor of both Faith and practice, drove thousands into the deserts as the only place where they could follow what they believed to be the real discipline of the Christian life, and be undistracted in their lives of Christian devotion. We need to understand this movement which was no mere negative escape from the world but, in its own way, a positive witness. No-one who has read *The Desert Fathers* by Helen Waddell will ever again dismiss them as escapists. They were, many of them, men with a passion for God, a penetrating awareness of their own sinfulness, and a most sensitive love of their fellow-men. Kingsley's *Hypatia* contains a horrifying description of how such discipline as they observed could result in a murderous fanaticism. But beside it must be set Chrysostom's famous sermon on 'The Statues'. In A.D. 387 a mob in Antioch destroyed the statues of the Emperor Theodosius and his family. This was *lése majesté* with a vengeance. The city was soon in a terror for it knew that the emperor had a quick temper and that a terrible punishment was certain. Chrysostom, in his sermon, preached after the emperor had pardoned the city, reminded his congregation how, when all the leading personalities had fled into the desert to escape, the monks from the desert had come into the city and by their importunity had swayed the verdict of the commissioners. Chrysostom, in fine rhetorical vein, says that 'the whole inhabited world will hear that the hermits of Antioch are men of apostolic courage'. In more senses than one the monks of the desert left the world to save the world.

One such hermit in Italy, Benedict by name, born just fifty years after the death of Augustine of Hippo, attracted a band of monks around him for whom he drew up a Rule which was to be the basis of the monasticism of the Middle Ages. This was a way of corporate living which was to prove of fundamental importance for the civilisation of Western Europe, a major factor in turning not a few 'bad princes' into godly rulers. It also communicated a way of life which enabled an illiterate peasantry and an equally illiterate order of feudal nobility to catch a glimpse of what the gospel was all about. What is important to note is that here we have the beginning of something quite new in the story of how the great commission was carried out. Here was a voluntary association dedicated to a specific way of representing the gospel. It was the essence of the monastic rule that a man or woman submitted to it voluntarily. Here in germ was the much later idea of the great missionary orders such as the Dominicans, Franciscans, then Jesuits and how many others, and, within another Christian tradition, the missionary societies. But all that is a later part of our story.

A book that shaped history

The second response to an unprecedented situation was the writing of a book. In A.D. 410 Alaric the Goth sacked Rome. It was the beginning of the 'Dark Ages' of Western Europe. One by one the traditional lights of Europe began to go out. What had been a fixed point of reference in the thinking of Western man for half a millennium had disappeared. New Rome on the Bosphorus never took the place of Old Rome on the Tiber. What really took the place of Old Rome was an Idea. And this idea was expressed in a book which has shaped Christian thinking ever since — Augustine's immortal *De Civitate Dei*, 'The City of God'. This magnificent expression of faith in God as the God of history, prompted by the sack of Rome, was not written from a safe refuge in North Africa. The Vandals were at the gate. Augustine died on August 28th, 430. Within a year Hippo was sacked.

The thesis of *De Civitate Dei* is that throughout all human history there have been two societies. The primary distinction for Augustine is not that between Church and State but rather, as J.N. Figgis defines it, 'between the Church and the world'. And as Figgis also makes clear the *Civitas Dei* 'is not the visible Church'. It is the *communio sanctorum,* what Augustine himself calls 'That most glorious society and celestial city of God's faithful' — a sentence so felicitously echoed in the Holy

Communion Service in the Book of Common Prayer as 'the blessed company of all faithful people' united in the mystical Body of the Son of God.

In a letter to Marcellinus, the Imperial Commissioner in North Africa, Augustine writes what not only summarises his interpretation of history but is also his bold assertion of faith even amidst what looks like the ruin of the world —

> God is the unchangeable Governor as he is the unchangeable Creator of mutable things, ordering all events in His providence until the beauty of the completed course of time, the component parts of which are the dispensations adapted to each successive age, shall be finished, like the grand melody of some ineffably rare master of song.

Within a century and a half, when it was very dark indeed, a Christian poet, Venantius Fortunatus, celebrated the mystery of Christ triumphant on the tree of the Cross in his great hymn, *Vexilla Regis*. We sing it as the hymn, 'The Royal Banners forward go'. So the great commission was carried on.

CHAPTER 3

From the Battle of Badr to the Capture of Constantinople by the Turks A.D.624 - A.D.1453

THE BATTLE OF Badr has rarely been listed among the decisive battles of the world, but it has a better claim to that title than some which have been so described.

Muhammad had set out from Medina with 300 men to meet a somewhat larger force from Mecca marching to attack him. By clever tactics he won a decisive victory. This began that astonishing career of conquest which, within less than one hundred years, took the armies of Islam deep into France, penetrated to central Asia, and invaded India.

Six centuries later that engaging world-traveller Ibn Battuta, born in Tangier in 1304, visited not only all North Africa and the Middle East but reached China, India, the Maldive Islands, and East Africa. On his last journey he crossed the Sahara to 'the land of the blacks'. On the way, he stopped at a town, Sijilmasa, where he stayed with a man whose brother he had met in China! Ibn Battuta was, thus, able to describe a religious community wider in extent than any other until the expansion of the Christian Church in the nineteenth century.

Failure in mission

This is the perspective within which we can best begin to see the Christian Church of the Middle Ages, a view not often attempted. In following the bitter-sweet story of how that Church obeyed the great commission it is again well that we should taste the truth when it is bitter. For the truth about the encounter of the Christian Church with Islam is bitter.

That curious perversion of piety, a mixture of religious

hysteria and sheer buccaneering, which we call the Crusades, was hardly calculated to present the Cross as a better symbol than the Crescent. Among the crusaders there were indeed men of the deepest piety. The concern for the Holy Places in Palestine was not mere superstition. There was, in medieval religion, a genuine desire to walk in the footsteps of Jesus, for men and women to identify themselves with his life and passion. The occupation of the Holy Places by unbelievers was felt to be a scandalous affront to the Christian Faith. But, somehow, the spirit of Jesus was sadly missing. A small illustration can be eloquent of an attitude of mind. In Jerusalem the Order of St. John had founded a hospital to be at once a hostel for pilgrims and a place for the sick. When the brief period of that Christian kingdom ended the hospital became a Muslim institution of which it is recorded that 'Christian pilgrims were still admitted on payment of two Venetian pennies, a courtesy which, in Christian days, had never been extended to Muslims'. The parable of the Good Samaritan was once again disconcertingly demonstrated.

The record, however, is not wholly dark. There were intimations of another attitude, a thread of real obedience running through the period. One and another had a vision unseen by most. Ramon Lull, for instance, whose life just overlapped that of Ibn Battuta, was himself no mean traveller. In his concern to present Christ to Muslims he travelled across North Africa, the Middle East, and reached the borders of India. In 1276 he founded at Miramar a college for the study of Arabic. He saw clearly the barrenness of the Crusades. In a prayer of meditation he pointed a better way — 'It appears to me, O Lord, that the conquest of that sacred land will not be achieved...save by love and prayer and the shedding of tears as well as blood... Let the knights become religious, let them be adorned with the sign of the Cross and filled with the grace of the Holy Spirit, and let them go among the infidels to preach truth concerning thy passion.' That was good New Testament. Ramon Lull sealed his faith by martyrdom in the town of Bugia in 1315. Sixteen years later, Ibn Battuta on his pilgrimage to Mecca probably passed through Bugia. One wonders if he heard of that killing. Had they ever met the two men would have found much in common.

In a more unsophisticated style Francis of Assisi had already anticipated Ramon Lull's concern to preach the Gospel to Muslims. In 1219 the dramatic contrast between his humility and courtesy and the undisciplined savagery of the crusaders, won the respect of the Sultan whose response was a free pass for Francis to visit Bethlehem. That is one more tantalising glimpse of what can happen when the Great Commission himself is allowed to appear in those whom he has commissioned.

Parallel to this devoted preaching of the Gospel by men like Lull and Francis was a remarkable anticipation by eight hundred years of one major activity of the Christian Mission in the twentieth century. Early in the twelfth century Peter the Venerable, eighth Abbot of Cluny, assembled a panel of learned men, including one Muslim, and set them to translate the Qur'an into Latin. In his preface to the work which was completed in 1141 Peter assured Muslims that 'he came bearing words, not weapons; that he dealt in reason not force; that he was prompted by love not hatred'. The same man also commissioned a translation of the Talmud into Latin. Here was a clear awareness that if you are to get near to a man of another Faith you must first take the trouble to discover what it is that he believes.

There was, indeed, sweetness in the bitter record of the medieval Christian approach to Islam. But one more bitterness must be recorded. Twice in the late thirteenth century, Kublai Khan, ruler of the Mongols, sent messengers to the Pope requesting missionaries — 'send me one hundred men skilled in your religion —... And so I shall be baptised, and then all my barons and great men, and then their subjects. And so there shall be more Christians here than there are in your parts.' Only two Dominicans were sent and they, unworthy members of a great missionary order, got as far as Armenia and then feared to go further. In the sequel, while some Mongols turned to Buddhism the majority became Muslims. It was as Muslims that they surged down into the Middle East and provided the impetus which finally carried the Turks triumphantly into Constantinople in 1453.

It is a strange story of an extraordinary opportunity thrown away. Apathy and ignorance had their share, as had the Pope's preoccupations with problems in Europe. As important were the fratricidal divisions among Christians. Latin-speaking Catholics, Greek-speaking Orthodox, Syriac-speaking Nestorians, could find no unity in the Christ they had in common. Plenty of non-religious factors, mostly political, also combined to paralyse any corporate attempt to carry out the great commission.

We do well to ponder history. It is not always a 'cordial for drooping spirits'. Fortunately the patience of God is never finally frustrated. He is always the God of the unexpected.

To China and the margins of the west

In the year 635 a Persian bishop, Alopen, was welcomed to the capital of the then greatest empire on earth, China. The full, complex fascinating story of that first Nestorian penetration of the Christian Faith into China can best be read in John Foster's book *The Church of the T'ang Dynasty*. Here we will turn rather to another event which took place that same year. A monk of Iona arrived at the capital of a small barbarian kingdom in Northumbria. This is a good starting point at which to begin our study of the response of the Church of western Europe to the barbarian invasions during the 'Dark Ages', from the fifth to the tenth centuries.

First, however, let us look at the contrast between the experience of the Apostle Paul and such a missionary as Aidan from Iona. Paul, we know, saw himself as put in trust with a timeless gospel, always and everywhere relevant, however variously dispensed whether in the form of milk or meat. In other respects he was a Spirit-inspired opportunist. Consider the circumstances in which he operated. He moved out into a world governed by a universal system of law and order. Society was disciplined in the use of one *lingua franca*, Greek. A sophisticated system of commerce was based on well-maintained communications on land and sea. Best of all, from Paul's point of view, there were dispersed throughout that world colonies of Jews, veritable salt in a savourless society. These colonies had for long attracted people to themselves by a

teaching and a way of life in which Paul himself had been born
and bred. Wherever he went, therefore, he had ready-made
points of contact. And with all this he had the good fortune to
be a man at home in two worlds, a Jew of impeccable
antecedents and also a Roman citizen.

Now, what we have to understand is that not one single one
of these circumstances was to be found in those Dark Ages in
which the great commission had to be obeyed. I have cited this
contrast because with our tidy and logical western minds we
tend to work to stereotypes. We talk about Paul's missionary
methods as though Paul's circumstances were universal. We
insist on certain principles by which to judge the distribution
of the Church's resources in man-power and money, unwilling
to accept the fact that the wind of the Spirit blows where he
wills, and we cannot tell the direction until we meet it in some
special circumstance. Moreover, that present circumstance is
most unlikely to be the same among the Indians of the High
Andes and the Indians of the Gangetic plain. Yet the gospel is
needed equally in both places. For effective obedience to the
great commission the one thing supremely needed in every age
is a lively response of Spirit-inspired opportunism, ever alert to
the certainty that God will provide different opportunities in
different circumstances.

The missionaries who evangelised the barbarians of Western
and Northern Europe, between the years 500 and 1000, faced
novel circumstances. They met the challenge in their own
inimitable way without slavery to one method. Consider how
different were the patterns of the missionary monasticism of
the Celtic Church and that developed in Italy.

Celtic monasticism was loosely organised almost as a family
affair. Christian villages were established, often as part of an
existing village. There was no rule of celibacy. Some monks
and priests were celibate, some were married. Scattered over
wide areas in thinly populated country, they adapted themselves to the tribal structure around them. This tribal structure
they sought to modify by a serious attempt to follow the
Mosaic pattern in ancient Israel. It was a remarkable experiment in spreading the Faith by contagion. Out from this

loosely organised social structure poured that astonishing company, Aidan, Columba, Ninian, Cuthbert, Columbanus and
Gall and many another to traverse all Britain and much of
Europe. Others, unnamed for the most part, sailed some of the
most tempestuous waters in the world in their fantastic little
coracles, and brought the Faith to the Shetlands and Iceland,
and, if legend tells truth, even to Greenland and North
America.

In sharp contrast to this ebullient individualism was the
strongly disciplined monasticism which derived from the
creative mind of Benedict of Nursia. Born about 480, Benedict,
as we have seen, was the heir of the discipline of Rome, whose
imperial grandeur had not yet faded from the minds of men. It
was, therefore, for a disciplined community's life of prayer,
study and hard manual labour that he designed his Rule. It met
the need of the moment. The monastic movement from Italy
spread like wild-fire. In a disintegrating society men and
women longed for sanctuary from primitive savagery. Yet
these monasteries were no mere 'escapes'. They were examples. They were a mirror of the gospel life. They provided
order. They were centres of education. They diffused culture.
Round them gathered the nucleus of a population from which
towns were to grow. Deserts blossomed, marshes were drained,
forests were contained. Ecology became a bearer of the gospel.
They were the seed-beds of a new civilisation.

But the monks of the Benedictine Rule were no less
concerned than their Celtic brethren to preach the gospel to the
heathen. Celtic monks were not the only ones addicted to
travel. A Boniface of Devon, Wilfrid and Willibrord of
Northumbria fruitfully grafted the Irish passion for travel on
to the more disciplined fabric of the Benedictine tradition.
They laid the foundation of the Christian Church in the
Rhineland and Frisia. Anskar from Picardy pioneered the
Gospel in Westphalia, Jutland and Sweden.

The message as proclaimed

What was the message these men, Celtic or Benedictine, proclaimed? It is difficult to trace the answer in any detail. They
were preaching to a people whose religion, fundamentally,

was pantheistic. Their natural world was peopled and controlled by unknown powers. Every tree had its spirit, every lake
its demon, every mountain its god. From what evidence we
possess, their point of attack was on this polytheism or rather
poly-demonism. Sometimes they attacked with the vigour of an
Elijah: sometimes with the mockery of Isaiah: rarely, it would
seem, with gentle reasoning. But always they preached One
God as the Creator, and Jesus Christ as the all-powerful
Saviour.

In one respect the barbarians were in a measure ready for the
message. These wandering barbarians were coming into contact with a more ordered world. For generations many of them
had served in Roman armies. Psychologically speaking there
was a deep disquiet engendered by the inadequacy of their old
Faith to give them any security in this new world.

The same factor has played a very large part in the
mass-movements of pagans into the Christian Church in Africa
in the twentieth century. Seeking power for living, the pagan
finds the needed power in the God of the Christians. To see
this is not only to see how God fulfils his purpose in many
ways. It may also be a reminder that in our twentieth century,
with its own so widespread a sense of insecurity, a gospel
which presents a power for living, which offers a new pattern
in which life can be organised, may well be on the very brink
of its greatest missionary opportunity, not least in our semi-
Christianised Western world.

The term 'semi-Christianised' deserves some scrutiny.
There is a legitimate sense in which Western Europe in the
High Middle Ages could in a strictly limited sense be called
Christendom. We will see the degree of that legitimacy in due
course. But it is sheer illusion to think of Europe at any stage in
its history as having been Christianised otherwise than in a
very superficial sense.

Tribal chiefs, for good reasons or bad, opted for the
Christian God. Their followers entered the waters of baptism
in loyalty to their chiefs and not because they had understood
what Paul meant about baptism in the sixth chapter of his letter
to the Romans. What happened in the Europe of the Dark Ages

was the mere beginning of a vast educational programme, which has not yet been completed, the slow, very slow, progress from a diet of milk to something a little more substantial. Is 'semi-Christianised' an altogether unfair summary of a record which has to include the Crusades, the Inquisition, religious wars between Christians, pogroms, the Atlantic slave-trade, the 'dark satanic mills', economic injustice, Auschwitz and Hiroshima, and the blood-letting in Vietnam and Northern Ireland? Surely this long record of savagery justifies 'semi-Christianised' as far as the Western world is concerned.

We do well to be very modest in our claims for the missionary enterprise, even if there is another side to the picture. We are better employed in adoring wonder at the patience of God. That he still believes in his Church is possibly the most amazing wonder of all.

Missions from the Eastern Churches

Even if we can take heart and hope from the real achievements of the Medieval Church in Western Europe we must not overlook the very great missionary enterprise of the Churches of the East. The Orthodox, Nestorian, Monophysite, Armenian Churches, for all their quarrelling were every whit as adventurous as the Church of the West. We have noted the Nestorians and others reaching as far as China. Whole tribes in Siberia became Christian in this period. Missionaries had certainly reached India and Ceylon by the early sixth century, and probably very much earlier. At the council of Nicea in 325 there was present a bishop from 'the Churches of the whole of Persia and great India'. Geographical terms used in those days are notoriously unreliable. But it is possible that there were Christian outposts in Sind in North-Western India. There is, also, the legend of St. Thomas which no Indian will allow to be other than a fact! It could be true.

Meanwhile in two other directions there was explicit obedience to the great commission. The southern Slavs, north of the Black Sea, were evangelised in the ninth century by two brothers Cyril and Methodius, building as they did on the faithful witness of Christian slaves who had been in those regions for at least five centuries.

Then, there was the southward movement. Two prisoners of war, Frumentius and Edesius, had introduced Christianity to Ethiopia in the fourth century. But the main expansion of the Faith down the Nile valley gained its chief impetus in the reign of the emperor Justinian (527-565). Nubia became a Christian kingdom and survived as such until at least the end of the fourteenth century, and Christians were still there in the sixteenth century. Then Islam finally overwhelmed the Christian Church. Why? Was part of the reason that two rival Christian traditions, the Orthodox and the Monophysite, had competed for the allegiance of the people, thus presenting a divided Church to a united Islam?

Nevertheless, whether in east or west, there is ample evidence that all through these centuries there were never lacking some whose eyes were on distant horizons, and who remembered that their commission was to the ends of the earth.

In history and with history

This is, perhaps, the point at which to make an interpretation which distinguishes between the Church as portrayed in this and the following chapters and the Church previously considered, before the sack of Rome in 410. I would attempt the distinction in this way. Up till the fourth century it is possible to describe the Church as suffering *in* history. The Church, then, was continually under threat of persecution, a victimised Church, not all that less a victim when, towards the end, it was patronised by the fourth century emperors. But, after this period and down until the twentieth century, we can describe the Church as suffering *with* history. That is to say that now it was organically related to the forces shaping history, to the creation of a civilisation, and to spreading that civilisation on a world scale. The Church of these centuries shared in all the pains of growth and change, moulding and moulded by its political, social and economic environment.

This might be put in another way by saying that, while drawing great inspiration from the witness of the Church of the early centuries, we must avoid identifying our circumstances with theirs. Jesus Christ, our living Lord, is *our* contemporary as he was *theirs*. But the saints and heroes of those early years are not our contemporaries in the same sense at all. We may and should rejoice with them in 'that blest communion, fellowship divine' in which the Church triumphant and the Church militant are one, both being 'in Christ'. Nevertheless those early warriors lived in a world of ideas and experience as remote from ours as theirs was from that of the ancient patriarchs of Israel. We need to keep this distinction clear if we are to grapple with the problems of our own age, and to see clearly how we in our turn are to be faithful to the Great Commission himself. That we can be faithful, is due precisely to the assurance that he is *our* contemporary.

Evangelism in depth

With that interpretation in mind let us look further, and at some depth, at the task facing the Church of the Middle Ages. Obedience to the great commission means a great deal more than activity on geographical frontiers. We do well to remember that the missionary who said 'Woe to me if I do not preach the gospel' (1 Cor. 9:16 R.S.V.) also aimed to 'compel every human thought to surrender in obedience to Christ' (2 Cor. 10:5). Further, it was his ambition 'to admonish everyone without distinction...instruct everyone in all the ways of wisdom, so as to present each one...a mature member of Christ's body' (Col. 1:28). Paul saw all this as part of the great commission and it still is.

Bringing every thought into captivity to Christ means going deep below men's conscious thinking, down into the subconscious and the unconscious. This deep penetration is very slow work. It was slow in the Middle Ages. It is slow still. But this also is evangelism.

We need to attempt a deep understanding of the mind of medieval man if we are to grasp the nature of the Church's task. We must try to appreciate his passion for pilgrimage, his obsession with miracles, his extravagant devotion to the saints, his credulity about their relics all of which gave focus to his devotion. These factors so utterly remote from twentieth-century thinking, gave infinite scope for roguery and for clerical exploitation. But that is by no means the whole picture. Freud, Jung and their successors have taught us much

about the undiscovered continents submerged below the level
of consciousness. We know that we are not quite so modern as
we think we are. We are not all that far away from the
caveman, the sabre-toothed tiger, and fear of the dark.
Medieval man was the same. Ancient fears and taboos,
inherited customs and ways of thought, are common to our
medieval predecessors and ourselves. Perhaps their idiosyncra-
cies were part of that ignorance at which, for a time, God
'winked' (Acts 17:30 A.V.). After all, the deep unconscious of
medieval man was as pagan as that of the philosophers of the
Areopagus or of the Phrygians of Galatia who were quite
prepared to worship Barnabas as Jupiter and Paul as Mercury.
God has a way of honouring very simple untutored faith,
which is just as well for all of us.

The signal faith of the Middle Ages was that God, through
Christ and his saints, was engaged on the work of salvation at
every level of man's being.

Pilgrims, miracles, relics

Pilgrimages may well have been 'walk-abouts', pleasant
escapes from the narrow horizons of the village community.
But in an age of religious sensitivity they had also an important
part to play. The hard and difficult pilgrimage to Jerusalem
showed the pilgrim the places associated with Christ and the
Gospel saints. This made for a more personal, more literal,
understanding of his faith. When he bathed in the Jordan he
knew himself very near his Saviour and perhaps glimpsed a
little more of the meaning of his baptism.

At a very simple level there is a delightful picture of that
very garrulous pilgrim, one Margery Kempe. She was not the
last of her kind, those who never quite know when to stop
talking. She was one of a party of English pilgrims, and she
rapidly exasperated her companions. At one point they deliberately lost her. But she caught up with them. They, however,
brusquely insisted that 'ye shall not speak of the Gospel...but
ye shall sit still, and make merry as we do'. It was no good! Her
habit of quoting passages from the Bible led to a final break
with the other pilgrims. How splendidly true to life. We have
all known ladies like that, and men too, and perhaps have been

a little ashamed at being so inarticulate ourselves. At least the
tale bears evidence that the Bible was being used evangelisti-
cally, if with a zeal lacking something of discretion.

The medieval obsession about miracles needs a sympathetic
understanding. There was then a total unawareness of the
causal nature of events. Many an acclaimed miracle would
have been no more than the response to a change of circumstance. Piety would exaggerate what had happened by way of
honouring a saint.   And there were always those ready to
exploit this devotion for unworthy ends. At the same time we
must not underestimate the reality of spiritual healing in many
a medieval miracle. Prayer and faith, when they coincide with
God's good will for the individual, have always been effective.
Psychosomatic healing cannot be explained away in materialistic terms. The Middle Ages were not so very wrong in
believing in the supra-natural, even if in their enthusiasm they
often gave the wrong diagnosis.

How crude they were about relics! Yes, but they were not
the last souvenir hunters! The medieval man's reverence for
relics was, at bottom, an insistence on the reality of things
unseen. An illustration here may help. I possess no relics in the
medieval understanding of the word. But in my home we are
surrounded by 'memorials' of one kind and another which
speak to us of people we have loved and continue to love. And
there are also many reminders of places hallowed in memory.
Who can measure what such modern 'relics' do in the deep
places of our being? Even a china jug with the legend 'a present
from Blackpool' may recall the magic of a holiday. So it was in
the Middle Ages. If, as someone has put it, 'Grace is the great
God himself permeating the unconscious', we may expect him
to use our imagination in recognising his grace and the joy of
the gospel.

But before leaving the miraculous it is legitimate in another
way to consider the monuments to the miraculous in the great
cathedrals of the Middle Ages, those miracles in stone,
Chartres, La Chapelle, Lincoln and Durham, to mention but
four out of hundreds. Our spirits soar upwards with the spire of
Salisbury Cathedral. Can we doubt that the spirits of the
architect and his workmen also soared, and, like ours, got
nearer heaven? Perhaps too often medieval man missed the

supernatural in the natural, as so many do to-day. Yet we can properly claim that those aspirations in stone were supernaturally inspired.

The Bible

Another aspect of the Middle Ages is frequently underestimated, its passion for learning, and in particular a passion for the study of the Bible. Probably there was as much devoted Biblical scholarship in those centuries as in any other period in the history of the Church, even if it lacked our modern apparatus. But lack of apparatus did not discourage the medieval exegete. Among such men was Hugh of St. Victor who, as Beryl Smalley so finely puts it, 'had that curiosity which set explorers in quest of Eldorado and led to the discovery of a continent'. He and his colleagues had the courage and imagination to seek guidance from Jewish scholars to the most accurate understanding of many passages in the Old Testament. There is something very modern when, writing about Biblical truth, Andrew of St. Victor can say

How hidden is truth, how deep she dwells, how far she screens herself from mortal sight... She hides, yet so as never wholly to be hidden! Careful seekers find her, that, carefully sought, she may again be found. None may draw her forth in her completeness, but by degrees. The fathers and forefathers have found her; something is left for the sons and descendants to find. So always: she is sought; something is still to seek; found, and there is something still to find.

That too is medieval religion.

While still on the subject of the Bible it is important to remember that right through this period, paraphrases of Scripture passages in prose and verse were widely used. By the end of the twelfth century came a demand for the Scriptures in the vernacular, a demand generally unwelcome to the authorities but quite irresistible. Over the next two centuries large portions of the Bible were known in fourteen European languages, of which the earliest German translation and the English translation inspired by John Wycliffe were the most pregnant for the immediate future. Before the age of printing, however, a Bible in the home was quite impossible. No nation could then be described as 'a people of one book and that book the Bible'. And even with the arrival of printing it was still a novelty when in 1804 the Bible Society was founded on the principle that in its own right the Bible was a major instrument in discharging the great commission.

In thus sympathetically surveying some aspects of the Middle Ages, either misunderstood or ignored, no attempt is intended at idealising the thousand years of our present study. Life then, as in much earlier times, was often 'nasty, brutish and short'. There was much wickedness in high places in Church and State as well as among ordinary folk. It can only by courtesy be called an 'age of faith'. All this has been fully documented almost *ad nauseam.* What is commonly overlooked is the never-failing effort by good men and women of every kind to discover more about God and the meaning of obedience to Christ and his commission.

The political fabric

If this period is to be understood in some of its most far-reaching impact upon the centuries ahead, attention must be paid to its political architecture and the bearing which this had upon the Church, her creed, and her obedience.

We may judge, and judge correctly, that the Church took the wrong turning in accepting Caesar so largely on his own terms. Whether or not Moltmann is fair in saying that 'from Justinian at the latest the Caesars conquered the Church', there is truth in what he goes on to point out, that increasingly God came to be pictured almost exclusively in terms of his omnipotence, his perfection, and his infinite distance from man, making necessary thereby a whole host of intermediaries. It is, indeed, a theological irony that the Church which refused to worship Caesar as God, came, to so large an extent, to worship God so much in the image of Caesar.

Nevertheless this is only a partial truth. Society is infinitely complex and if anarchy is to be avoided unity has to be sought.

The anarchic elements in the Middle Ages need no further elucidation here. One task of the Church was to achieve a unity in which order would triumph over chaos. Two great Popes, Gregory VII (1073-1085) and Innocent III (1198-1216) did for a time succeed in creating an ordered society which could merit the name of Christendom.

Without at all minimising the price subsequent generations had to pay for this attempt at totalitarianism in the organisation of a Church-dominated society, it is important to see what was being attempted. It was not just the lust for power pursued to inordinate lengths. Within that medieval world it was a genuine attempt to establish order and justice. That is no ignoble ideal. Furthermore it has firm Biblical roots. At the very heart of the Old Testament, and by no means overlooked in the New Testament, lies the conviction that the righteousness of God must find its reflection in justice among men. How such a reign of justice is to be realised is as much a problem of the twentieth century as it was of the eleventh and thirteenth. Our problems are global and their solution must be attempted in a religiously pluralistic world. But a measure of respect is due to that serious attempt once made, even though on a much smaller scale. The continual refrain of the prayers of the Middle Ages that there might be peace so that the Church could discharge her mission is an eloquent reminder that chaos is rarely conducive to communicating the gospel.

Tensions

What we must also recognise in the Middle Ages is that the centralisation of authority, the principle of order, was always in tension with cross-currents which found expression in regional and local interests. The tension between order and freedom of local initiative is perennial. This period might appear superficially to exemplify a marvellous synthesis of Church and State. That was indeed one part of the fabric of medieval society. But another part was represented by the popularity of pilgrimages; the socially disruptive impact of the Crusades; the intrusive energies of the friars, rarely if ever under central control; the emergence of universities where men learnt to ask awkward questions; the economic revolution of the growth of towns. All of these were formidable elements making for local initiatives and creating a taste for liberty. It proved to be the nascent nationalisms, and neither the Holy Roman Empire nor the Papacy, which learnt to exploit them. This, in more ways than one, was to be of great significance for the pattern taken by obedience to the great commission in the next period.

Passing attention must be paid to one feature of the scene in this period which popularly focussed much of this 'resistance' to centralisation. This was the enormous influence of preaching which took the form of satire and complaint. By the fourteenth and fifteenth centuries this had become the norm of preaching. It was at once a protest against the corrupt leadership of the ecclesiastical hierarchy and of the clergy generally, religious and secular; an expression of despair at economic conditions; terror at the afflictions of the Black Death; and bitterness at the chronic conditions of banditry and war. Little of this preaching included any recognisable gospel. Rather it was a very rough attempt to express what today would be called a 'theology of liberation'. Only, perhaps, by the Waldensians and Hussites and, in England, by Langland and Wycliffe and the Lollards was a note struck which sounded like the gospel.

There is a nice passage in *Piers Plowman* in which Langland can be seen as anticipating Bunyan. A great company of men are seen asking the way to find truth. And it is Piers Plowman who points the road

> They must go through Meekness till they come to Conscience: next cross the brook called Be-buxom-of-speech by the ford called Honour-your-fathers. Pass by Swear-not-in-vain and Covet-not by Steal-not and Slay-not, over the bridge of Pray-well where Grace is the gate-keeper and Amend-you is his assistant, and then through the narrow gate to paradise.

The Great Isolation

One final note on this period brings us back to the point from which we started — the triumphant progress of Islam. An important effect of the range of Islamic conquests, to which the effect of the schism with the Orthodox Church of the East must be added, was to make Western Europe, in fact, a cultural and religious island. The visible success in the conversion of the barbarians, a genuine measure of unity in faith, the synthesis of Church and State which was real enough, all these combined to limit the horizons of Western theological thinking. It led to a presumptuous intellectual triumphalism which was wholly unaware of its essential insularity. We have noted the failure to attempt the conversion of Muslims and Jews, otherwise than by coercion. Exceptions to this were notable in being exceptions. The baleful effect of this isolationism in medieval theological thinking has dogged the theological learning of the West down into our own century. As a result we are only just beginning to see any kind of attempt to take seriously the claims of other great Religious Faiths as offering an alternative to the Christian Gospel. Furthermore this theological arrogance of the West played its own subtle part in the political, economic and cultural imperialism which so heavily compromised the Church's obedience to its great commission in the ensuing centuries.

CHAPTER 4

From the Little Ships of Diaz, Columbus and Da Gama to the Sinking of the Russian Fleet by the Japanese in the Straits of Tsushima A.D.1492 - A.D.1905

IN THE SECOND half of the fifteenth century a change came over the balance of power in the eastern Mediterranean. The commercial empire of Venice slowly dwindled. The trade routes from the East were increasingly closed. The Turks captured Constantinople. The other entrepots for trade, Beirut and Alexandria, were far more harshly controlled. Extortionate tolls, for instance, virtually closed the pilgrim traffic to Jerusalem from 1490-4. With all this Europe felt the pinch economically. Spices, particularly pepper, an exclusive product of the East, had become indispensable for European kitchens, just as, five hundred years later, oil had become indispensable for European industry. And it was not easy to come by.

A search for a new route to the east to satisfy the need for spices was one major factor in the expeditions of Diaz, Columbus, and da Gama between the years 1488 and 1497. This was not, however, the only motive for exploration. It was believed that somewhere in the East lay the kingdom of Prester John, a Christian prince. It was fondly hoped that, by linking up with him, it would be possible to launch a crusade to recapture the Holy Places and be the means of converting the peoples of Islam. It was exploration for mission as well as commerce.

On any reckoning a new age had begun. Obedience to the great commission faced a prospect of hitherto undreamt opportunity.

For our purpose, Christopher Columbus is the key figure. His achievement as an act of daring was matched by the depth of his Christian devotion. Readers who would get the full

flavour of his venturing across the Sea of Gloom, as the
Atlantic was then called, cannot do better than read Alistair
Cooke's *America*, where he describes how Columbus was
commissioned to prepare an expedition for 'Gospel and Gold'.

We seriously misjudge the age if we cynically dismiss the
precedence given to the word 'Gospel'. Thirty-three days after
leaving Cadiz, landfall was made on an island to which
Columbus gave the name San Salvador in token of his gratitude
to the Holy Saviour who had been his protector. Later in his
report, he speaks of the inhabitants as naked savages and adds 'I
myself gave them much and took nothing in return. I did this to
pacify them, and that they might be led to become Christians.
Let Christ rejoice in the salvation of the souls of so many nations
hitherto lost. Let us all rejoice, both for the exaltation of our
Faith and for the increase of our wealth'.

Unfortunately it was the last five words which really excited
Europe. Gold very quickly took precedence over Gospel, and
there began what Alistair Cooke grimly describes as 'the
longest, most determined, and most brutal gold-rush in history'. And so, just when it became possible for the first time for
witness to Christ to be made 'to the ends of the earth', Gospel
and Gold are found inextricably joined together. Cross the
centuries, and another Christian explorer, David Livingstone,
sees the hope of Africa to lie in 'Christianity and Commerce'.
The capital letters in each case stand for exactly the same
factors. Further be it noted that Livingstone's second journey
was financed by the British government, as Columbus' expedition had been by the Spanish government of Ferdinand and
Isabella.

We must be prepared as Christians to follow the next four
hundred years with very great humility and much searching of
heart. No attempt will be made here to enter into the details of
the story. It has been recorded extensively. More important for
our purpose is to see these centuries in perspective, and to note
the extent to which they inherited three legacies from the
Middle Ages. That entail has not yet been fully broken. There
is no understanding of the problems which had to be faced in
obeying the great commission, no appreciation of the gains and
losses experienced in that obedience without attention being
given to that entail.

We may describe the three legacies from the Middle Ages as follows—

1. Caesar and his conscience
2. The Gospel and the inner imaginings of European man
3. Triumphalism

Caesar and his conscience

In very simple terms we may say that what happened in the Middle Ages was that the Church tamed Caesar. In the process it gave Caesar a Christian conscience, indeed it was itself that conscience. In the process, the Church reduced chaos to a genuine order which men called Christendom. In a word the Church created Europe and European man and European civilisation.

Now, as far as Caesar was concerned, the main effect of the Renaissance and the Reformation was that Caesar took over responsibility for his own conscience. He was firmly of opinion that it should remain Christian. He was sure that there must be a moral basis for society if order was to be preserved. From the Middle Ages he derived the conviction that the indispensable basis for common order was a common Faith. But he was going to determine what that Faith was to be. This meant that the emerging national states were to have uniformity in religion. Faith and practice were to be determined by Caesar. And the theology to match this new self-assertion was a subtle development of one part of the medieval synthesis of Church and State. Caesar called this development the Divine right of Kings, and it was held equally tenaciously, whatever view Caesar took of the disruption of unity of Faith created by the Reformation.

No attempt can be made here to argue the relative merits of the rival theologies which emerged from the Reformation and the Counter-Reformation. Still less is there space to do more than note the significance of the radical positions taken up by 'the step-children of the Reformation'. These were those Christian groups whose revolutionary views, with a long medieval pedigree, were to undergird orthodox Dissent and, in due course, to make a significant contribution to the slow growth of constitutional democracy. It was, then, against the background of such political, social and theological confusion that the great commission in the first part of this period, was carried out.

Caesar was by no means indifferent to his responsibilities in this regard. When the Pope conveniently divided the newly discovered worlds between Spain and Portugal, the respective Caesars saw to it that their fleets carried missionaries, and that every effort was made to produce new Christians by force, if persuasion failed. In the first centuries of this era the story is an ugly one.

In England, we may note that the charter of the East India Company was quite explicit about the missionary objective, though much more pragmatically expressed. And when, later, a genuine missionary interest began to stir in the Churches in Britain, voluntary societies for this purpose, unrelated to commercial enterprises, had to have Royal Charters to make them legitimate. It was axiomatic for Caesar to wish that 'Foreign Missions' should be reckoned to be under his own ultimate direction. Things had moved a long way from the Middle Ages, but the continuity is unmistakable.

The gospel and the inner imaginings of European man

We have seen how formidable a task had to be undertaken by the medieval Church if the inner imaginings of men were to be brought into any semblance of obedience to Christ. Progress had been slow. It was to be no quicker in this period, when the imaginations of men had received so vast a stimulus, with so many new horizons to explore. Advance towards some control over the perennial fascination of gold has been very uneven. 'Trust in God and 5%', may have been an echo of the medieval doctrine about usury. But it was a very faint echo. Yet, as we shall see, some small progress has been made.

We have now to consider a very embarrassing inheritance from the Middle Ages. As far back as the *Epistle of Barnabas* we find the Devil portrayed as the 'Black One'. That may have had little significance, may have been no more than an identification of evil with fear of the dark. But the idea was ominous. Within a few centuries hermits, in pursuit of their goal of loneliness, pressed southward from Upper Egypt into an area where they encountered a population that was black. This encounter haunted their dreams and shaped many of their visions. Again and again we read of their temptations coming to them with the Devil disguised as a seductive black girl. Wrestlings with black men were also seen as wrestlings with the Devil. All this was faithfully reported by such writers as Cassian who, early in the fifth century, wrote up the material he had collected from conversations with the desert hermits. His *Conferences*, as he called his reports, became favourite reading in all the monasteries of western Europe in the Middle Ages. In this way a stereotype was created, suggesting that there was something inherently evil in blackness and, by association, in the black man. The next step was to think of the black man as sub-human and not having human rights.

That this stereotype was influencing the European mind can be seen from what was probably Shakespeare's last play, *The Tempest* (1611-1612). 'Come on,' says Prospero to Miranda, 'We'll visit Caliban my slave, who never yields us kind answer.' Miranda replies 'Tis a villain, sir, I do not love to look on.' Prospero insists, 'We cannot miss him: he does make our fire, fetch in our wood; and serves in offices that profit us. What ho! Slave! Caliban! Thou earth, thou! speak.' There is much else in the same vein. And we watch Caliban enslaved to liquor. He takes leave of the play with words strangely prophetic of black Africa's contemporary response to the white man— 'What a thrice-double ass was I, to take that drunkard for a god, and worship this dull fool.'

Hawkins had lifted his first cargo of 300 slaves from the coast of Sierra Leone in 1562, just fifty years before, providing useful dramatic material for Shakespeare.

All the horrors of the Atlantic slave trade, in which Hawkins joined, were to shape Europe's contact with Africa for the next three hundred years. That legacy has vitiated the relationships of the white man with the black man, and indeed with any coloured man, ever since. No small part of the explosiveness behind racial bitterness today derives from the same source. The Devil has had a long innings with the unconscious of European man. Laurens Van Der Post's *The Dark Eye in Africa* is a brilliant insight into the white man's dilemma. This, and Philip Mason's *Prospero's Magic* are indispensable reading for anyone who doubts the validity of the picture I have painted, and who, being white, wants to understand himself.

In this tragic historic clash of colour has been found, and is still found, a major obstacle to the progress of the gospel. But the record is not all shadow. On one count the missionaries who went to Africa, whatever their other blunders, were uncompromising. They insisted that there was nothing in the world which the African could not achieve if he was given the opportunity. They believed this when nobody else believed it. And they acted on their belief. And the white missionary proved his case. He it was who demonstrated that 'Black is Beautiful', long before anyone else dreamt of such an idea. It was the missionary who began to disinfect colour of its lasting stain. If we may take Isaiah 45:3 (A.V.) out of context, but without apology, it was the missionary, not the anthropologist, whose faith first uncovered the 'treasures of darkness, and hidden riches of secret places'.

Triumphalism

We have seen earlier how the isolation of Europe, hemmed in by Islam in a crescent-shaped threat from Spain to the Balkans, and threatened by Slavonic tribes and invading hordes from Asia, became introverted in its thinking about itself, entirely self-sufficient in its theology, and united in the untempered conviction that it possessed a monopoly of civilisation.

Now, suddenly, with those little ships, Europe discovered the wider world, but unfortunately viewed it with myopic eyes. With ceaseless momentum and breath-taking success the new world was exploited commercially. The political and cultural invasion was much more gradual but, in the end, scarcely less dramatic. The unquestioned assumption of European man remained the same as that of his medieval predecessors, that Europe and European ways were the acme of civilisation. An equally unexamined assumption, but a much more serious one for the great commission, was that the Christian Faith could only be exported with its European trappings. It took centuries for this fundamental arrogance to be recognised, even by missionaries. If, today, there are still acute tensions between the Churches of the West and the Churches of the 'Third World', we need look no further than this arrogance, no less unpleasant when most unconscious, for an explanation.

The four-fold pattern

The four-fold pattern — preaching, teaching, healing and witness — was maintained throughout this period. Preaching took many forms, always declaratory, often argumentative, too often fiercely polemic; not always 'sweetly reasonable' and sympathetic. Teaching used all the available media. Healing was mainly of the *psyche*, liberating men and women from a life-time of bondage to primeval fears and some of the attendant diseases. Only at the end of this period was modern scientific medicine pioneered in many areas by Mission hospitals. Witness, personal and corporate, not without benefit of martyrdom, was continuous. However inadequately, the great commission was obeyed. The Church grew.

Here I will develop briefly only the one element of 'teaching'. Through education the missionary movement made its most momentous contribution to the future, at almost every level, social, economic and political, as well as evangelistic. Windows for the mind were opened through literacy. However we may judge the cultural invasion of the West, whether among tribal peoples in Africa and Latin America and in many other areas, or among the sophisticated races of Asia, this invasion did inexorably make towards one world, made 'conversation' possible on a world scale.

Literacy was necessary for any growth in understanding the Faith. And for many missionaries this meant the translation of the Bible into the vernacular. This was of far-reaching significance. Hundreds of languages were for the first time reduced to writing. And in all these the first reading material consisted of portions of the Bible and, in due course for many, the whole Bible. Christians in wide areas became 'the people of one book and that book the Bible'. In more sophisticated areas the Bible in the vernacular created a ferment in the great ethnic religions, initiating renaissance and reform, the ultimate issue of which is beyond our present seeing. There are more ways than one by which the Holy Spirit prepares men's minds for the gospel.

One intriguing illustration may suffice. In 1959 an African political leader, Ndabaningi Sithole, wrote a book with the title, *African Nationalism*, which contained an appreciative as well as critical appraisal of the missionary impact upon Africa. In it he quoted a conversation between two Africans, which ran like this — one was critical of the whole missionary enterprise — 'You see the missionary came here and said, Let us pray, and we closed our eyes, and when we responded Amen at the end of his prayer, we found the Bible in our hands, but lo! our land had gone.' To this the other African replied 'When Europeans took our country we fought them with our spears, but they defeated us because they had better weapons and so colonial power was set up much against our wishes. But lo! the missionary came in time and laid explosives under colonialism. The Bible is now doing what we could not do with our spears.'

Actually, the missionary and the Bible generally got there well before the European government. But the fuse, though slow burning, was none the less explosive for that. In Africa, at least, it is beyond contradiction that, when alien flags were run down, the new leaders in the independent countries had, with rare exceptions, received their primary, and often their secondary education in Christian schools, where the Bible had a special place in the curriculum! The God who works in history often uses our pious intentions in very unexpected fashion. As Isaiah once observed, God's thoughts are not like our thoughts nor his ways like our ways. We would save ourselves a lot of worry and be less anxious about steadying the ark of the covenant if we would accept this fact, and rejoice over it.

Colonialism

With the possible exception of the kingdom of Jerusalem established by the Crusaders, and surviving precariously from 1099-1244, the Middle Ages had no scope for colonial adventures. Colonialism is essentially a phenomenon of the expansion of Europe. But the word needs some definition. During much of our period, colonies were settlements of Europeans in either uninhabited or very thinly populated areas.

In common parlance that is not what is meant today by colonialism. As a 'hate' word, 'colonialism' refers to the experience by which an alien imperial rule was established, generally by force, over resentful and unwilling peoples. Nor was it necessary for an alien flag to be flown. Perhaps the most pernicious of all forms of colonialism was what Europeans established in China in the form of complete commercial control, without the acceptance of any moral responsibility whatever.

Colonialism, then, is an emotive word. It is impractical to imagine that, in any foreseeable future, the peoples of Africa and Asia and the oppressed majorities in Latin America will be able or willing to view objectively 'colonialism' as here defined. A few very remarkable writers, here and there in those countries, have achieved an astonishing objectivity. And there have been statesmen whose capacity to transcend their peoples' and their own humiliations has been miraculous. But we do well to accept the fact that 'colonialism' in every form is held to be a detestable crime committed by the white man, very specifically, the *white* man.

That, however, does not absolve us from the task of giving a brief assessment of 'colonialism' as a factor impinging upon the Christian Mission, for impinge it certainly did. And Christians, whatever their race, are committed to the Biblical faith that God is at work in history, that all history, therefore, is sacred history, even that which seems most secular. Our indispensable guide-book for this insight is the Old Testament. The people of Israel did not enjoy being the victims of imperialisms erupting from the valleys of the Nile and the Euphrates. But it was one of the great moments of history when an Israelite prophet, baffled by international events and the threat to the existence of his own nation, could understand God to be saying to him, 'I am raising up the Chaldeans' (Hab. 1:6). The enormous contribution which the Jews have made to the religious sensitivities of mankind look back to two of their finest moments: when one of their great prophets was able correctly to understand God as saying that the ruler who was to bring about the Babylonian captivity, Nebuchadrezzar, is 'my servant' (Jer. 25:9); and another prophet to describe the alien ruler, Cyrus, who was to end that captivity, as being 'my shepherd' (Isa. 44:28).

Until Western Christians are more familiar with the idea that Chairman Mao could prove to have been just such a servant of God's purposes, they will be wise to wait until African and Asian prophets point to the fulfilment of God's purposes in the white colonialisms of the past.

A few generalisations are all that can be attempted here. Because nineteenth century imperialisms enforced peace and order, they were naturally welcomed by the missionaries. Because these colonial regimes enforced tolerance for minority opinions they did provide an umbrella under the shade of which the very tender plant of many an African and Asian Church could take root and flourish. Inevitably, to the grave embarrassment of the real fulfilment of the great commission, the Church and Caesar could very plausibly be identified. This naturally encouraged the growth of nominal adherents. This, in turn, provided ample evidence of the immaturity of the local Christian Church and encouraged a delaying tactic by missionaries in developing self-supporting and self-governing Churches. And, very easily, spontaneous expansion withered away.

As I would insist, these are generalisations. In another context it would be easy to provide ample evidence of another side to this picture. But the above paragraph must stand if we are to recognise how little prepared were so many Christians in Africa and Asia, and so many foreign missionaries, for the gathering spirit of revolt against alien rule.

What happened when the Japanese navy sank the Russian navy in the Straits of Tsushima on May 27-28, 1905, although few realised it at the time, was the end of an era. And, it went out with a bang, not a whimper! For suddenly it became apparent that the white man was not, after all, invincible. An earth tremor shook Asia after that bang. Later, with the great European civil war of 1914-18 a similar tremor was felt in Africa. European seismographs for reading this kind of earthquake did not exist in Whitehall, in the Quai d'Orsay, in the Wilhelmstrasse, or at the Hague. All was quiet on Capitol Hill and in the State Department.

It is a matter of history that the protagonists of the Christian Mission had a better equipped leadership to understand what was happening. In the next chapter we shall see the instrument which they had to hand for grappling with the upheaval. But far too many Christians are still dizzy from the repercussions of that upheaval. Perhaps one of the most important questions which those who are committed to obeying the great commission have to ask themselves is this — Can we recognise and accept that a vast work of demolition is indispensable before a great work of construction can be undertaken? In a word can we trust in the God of hope; and let him fill us with all joy and peace by our faith in him, until, by the power of the Holy Spirit we overflow with hope? That was Paul's prescription (Rom. 15:13).

CHAPTER 5

From Man in the Air to Man on the Moon
July 25, 1909 - July 20, 1969

MAN HAS ALWAYS been a 'watcher of the skies', watching in wonder and expectancy. Was it birds flying high which first suggested strange possibilities to the minds of men? One great Hebrew with poetry in his soul, saw the exodus of his people from Egypt in no pedestrian terms. Rather, he saw God bringing his people out 'on eagles' wings' (Exo. 19:4). A careful bird-watcher carried the thought further. He saw God protecting his people like an eagle its young, watching over its nest, spreading its pinions and taking up its fledglings, carrying them on its wings (Deut. 32:11. See also Isa. 31:5).

In the Greek myths, poetry carried the idea adventurously forward with Daedalus and his son Icarus manufacturing wings in order to escape from prison. Much later, that prolific genius Leonardo da Vinci sketched out plans for a flying machine. So, for millennia, men watched and wondered.

At last, when the internal combustion engine had been invented, a Frenchman, Louis Blériot, landed at Dover on a July day in 1909. He had left Calais thirty-one minutes before, flying in a monoplane weighing 600 lbs with a 22 h.p. engine. For anyone with imagination those prosaic details are sheer poetry and courage.

What Blériot did that day was much more than the inaugurating of the air-age. He revolutionised man's perspective. Communication suddenly meant something entirely new. Before long, men would fly the Atlantic: a woman would fly solo to Australia. Neighbourhood slowly began to have a new meaning. And it proved to be a very constructive meaning. The

Flying Doctor Service in the Australian outback: the Missionary Aviation Fellowship in Africa: crop-spraying by air: aerial
surveys: rescues by helicopter: all these later commonplaces
became possibilities on July 25, 1909.

But there were other latent developments. Did anyone in the
crowd at Dover that day remember his Shakespeare and, as he
looked out over the channel, wonder what the day portended
for England's 'moat defensive...against the envy of less happier
lands'? Thirty-one years later the moat still had some value,
but not much! Blériot cannot be blamed for the ruins of the
City of London through which I walked on my way to my
office, morning after morning from 1942-45. And he could not
be blamed for the ruins of Hamburg and Essen and Dusseldorf
which I was to see soon after the War. Later still, I was to visit
the scarred memorial of one aeroplane's visit to Hiroshima on
an August day in 1945. The world had certainly become a
neighbourhood, and with a vengeance.

Such were some of the vast changes in human consciousness
resulting from Louis Blériot's heroic achievement. No other
combination of human courage and human skill has so quickly and
so fatefully, and yet also so beneficially, shaped modern history.

Then, there was another July day when a young American,
Neil Armstrong, first put man's foot upon the surface of the
moon. On the morning after, the Leading Article in *The Times*
for July 21, 1969, had the headline 'Wonder of the World', and
saw the event as symbolic of 'man reaching out beyond his
previous confines'. Cautiously that leader-writer added—

This celebrated event is also most mysterious in its consequences. It may be little more than a brilliantly-lit blind
alley, a successful act of scientific curiosity, but also an
intrusion into an atmosphere so alien that it will remain of as
little use to man as the much more convenient exploration of
the polar regions. It could therefore be a step that leads little
further than itself or it could lead to a whole series of new
explorations, to a new way of life for man and not merely to
the satisfaction of his curiosity or the extension of his
psychological boundaries.

That was indeed a cautious forecast. But to get the full flavour of those closing words about the extension of man's psychological boundaries, we must join Louis Blériot's name with that of Neil Armstrong and look at the sixty years spanned by these men's achievements.

Space-ship earth

If, as Christians, we are at all to comprehend the world of the last quarter of the twentieth century: if, as in private duty bound, we have to look ahead and see how the great commission is to be spelt out in our present and our future, we must look very carefully at those sixty years. They held very unexpected developments.

Speaking in Westminster Abbey, an American astronaut was to use a phrase perhaps more pregnant than he knew. He spoke of 'Space-ship Earth'. Now a space-ship is a very congested area, as we all saw on the T.V. when the Russians and Americans had their dramatic rendezvous in space. And our earth is also becoming very congested. The most staggering development of those sixty years has been a biological one, the phenomenal growth in the world's population. This biological fact is probably a far greater threat to world peace than any nuclear war. Or it might be the cause of such. For with the growth of population there is not yet any commensurate growth in food production. More accurately, perhaps, we should say that the will to distribute fairly the food that is available does not yet exist. Combine hunger with under-employment: match these with the appalling contrast between the lush material prosperity of the industrially developed nations and the standards of living in the poor nations: and we need look no further for the basic cause of revolutionary tumult and ruthless terrorism. Beneath the surface of almost all the political events of this period, could we trace them to their roots, is just fear, fear *for* survival.

The extension of our psychological boundaries does not necessarily lead to heroic adventure. It can as easily lead to a longing to 'return to the womb', or a 'death wish'. Claustrophobia, as defined in a dictionary, is a 'morbid fear of confined spaces'. It will do very well as a description of the underlying sickness of humanity today. We are very uncomfortable on 'Space-ship Earth'.

Frankenstein

During the greater part of these sixty years this biological revolution was little noticed. Much more obvious was the amazing progress of technology. This has been almost hypnotic on the human mind. The scientifically-trained technician has become man's prophet and priest. He could be waiting in the wings to be announced as king. There appears to be no end to his inventiveness. He is the cause of the revolution of 'rising expectations' which is now universal.

But technology has created a Frankenstein of its own. This is not the science-fiction idea of a machine taking over control from man. The machine can, and often does, make a man redundant. The real Frankenstein is the sheer staggering complexity of the industrial and commercial world which seems to make all moral judgments impossible. So interdependent is the whole complex, nationally and internationally, that the individual's freedom to influence events is virtually negligible, even in the highest ranks of management. The multi-national company, with its operations completely impersonal, is the symbol of our dilemma.

We need to face these facts in all their bleakness. The great religions of mankind all emerged in societies dominated by agriculture. Industrial development was minimal. The individual's occupation was likely to be hereditary, in one form or another of a caste system. The individual would generally be significant not so much in himself as part of a carefully graded community. It was his place in that community which gave him his meaning. But, at least, these societies had a moral basis of mutual responsibility. Each individual had his worth. And this even applied to the slave. Paul could advise a slave how to behave to his master and the master how to behave to the slave because there was a direct human relationship between them. A moral relationship was possible. What kind of a relationship can the man on the shop-floor of a great factory, or a workman in a sub-contractor's business have with the managing directors of a multi-national company? It is the sheer impersonality of the organisation of society, and not the machine, which makes for inhumanity. To be humane you must be able to be human, and that involves a degree of freedom.

This is the new context within which the great religions have to function today. We will see, in due course, that the picture is not all shadows. There are lights in the darkness. But far too much religious moralising is being done in a vacuum. Communication does not take place. 'What can I, as an individual, do?' That is a real question and there is no easy answer.

Going deep down

While men were successfully imitating the birds and venturing into space, another exploration was taking place into the *terra incognita* of man's unconscious. The pioneers here were Sigmund Freud and Carl Jung. Enormous benefits have come from this exploration, an exploration far more significant for human living than the probing of space. We have come to know a great deal more about ourselves than we had known before. This in itself is good, even if the knowledge is not very pleasant. To become aware that all our righteousness is as filthy rags is a valuable bit of spiritual realism, and adds to our confidence in the diagnosis of the prophet Isaiah (Isa. 64:6 A.V.), of Paul and, above all, of Jesus himself. People who do not take Isaiah or Paul or Jesus seriously may arrive at the truth about themselves through Freud and Jung, although they will still need Isaiah and Paul and Jesus to find out what to do about themselves.

That Christian judgment is important. For we need to face realistically that this exploration can involve new dangers for the human spirit. The indoctrinated mind is no novelty. But, until the other day, the mind could always rebel. Today it can be so manipulated that no rebellion is possible. George Orwell's *Animal Farm* was neither satire nor fiction but an intelligent understanding of what can happen to the animal — Man.

The extension of our psychological boundaries also has another equivocal dimension. In these sixty years we have moved from the wireless of Marconi to Satellites, off which can be bumped pictures and information from the other side of the world straight into our living rooms. We now can have instant knowledge of events twelve thousand miles away. Unfortunately, instant knowledge rarely carries with it instant understanding. Often it will convey no meaning or just misunderstanding. Too much information which is not understood leads to apathy. And mental apathy can lead to being receptive to non-news. One can be anaesthetised by non-news, and so become very suggestible. Sub-liminal advertising is the latest assault on the human mind. George Orwell's 'Big Brother' may not be all that far away from our living rooms. Freud and Jung have made this crystal clear.

Social engineering

Now, all this rapid change of perspectives and the consequent social upheavals have meant that increasing attention has been directed to what is called social engineering. There is no space here to analyse all that has been, and is being, attempted under the labels of communism, democratic socialism, and nationalism. To begin with, these words all have multiple meanings. In some forms they represent a naked lust for power. That, after all, is latent in all attempts to manipulate men — including the religious. But, if we are to enter with sympathy into the minds of millions of people today, understand that they not only accept but welcome such social engineering, we must see that, for them, it is a concern for a better life, a dream of paradise regained. Nor are we justified in denying to all the engineers and planners a share in the same concern, the same dream. The Christian's duty is to scrutinise with care all such engineering, because human beings are not machines. Man is made in the image of God. And God is not a machine. But with that caveat the Christian must be actively involved in every attempt to secure a better and more just society.

One world

One most notable fact emerges from a study of the period spanned by our two July dates: and that is the emergence of a genuine sense in which all our problems are world-embracing. Two world-wars contributed to this new awareness, as have the subsequent world revolutions. This is one world.

The Greeks had a word for it — *oikoumene,* commonly translated 'ecumenical'. By it the Greeks meant 'the inhabited world', though they limited the inhabitants. The *oikoumene* did not include the barbarians, a considerable limitation. Later the word came to signify the Roman world, a much more comprehensive use of the word. Then, in its adjectival form, it came to be used of the great Christian Councils, which in so far as they aimed at being representative could genuinely claim to be, in intention, world-embracing.

Before, however, we come to see the significance of the Christian meaning of the word today, it is important to recognise and accept that the word, *ecumenical,* can apply quite properly to communism, to the economic order, to the United Nations and its subsidiary agencies, and to religions such as Buddhism, which today is explicitly world-embracing in its purpose, as, by definition, is Islam. Modern science can also claim the word. The mind of man is thinking globally. The Christian is not the only person with his eyes on 'the ends of the earth'. This should be a very great encouragement and equally a very great challenge.

Christians getting together

Like everything else that is of enduring significance to the Christian Faith, the ecumenical movement of our time finds its roots in the Bible and, more particularly, in the New Testament. In that deeply sensitive interpretation of our Lord's communion with his Father on the night of his arrest we see how deeply he was concerned with the unity of his disciples *and* of all those whom they would themselves disciple — 'May they all be one: as thou, Father, art in me, and I in thee, so also may they be in us, that the world may believe that thou didst send me' (John 17:21). Only a short while before, he had said, 'as I have loved you, so you are to love one another. If there is this love among you, then all will know that you are my disciples' (John 13:35).

Paul, who was nothing if not direct, hearing of factions in

the Church in Corinth, asked one devastating question, 'Was it Paul who was crucified for you?' (1 Cor. 1:13). That question ought to puncture all our denominational pride, all our sectarian substitutes for Christianity. That it has not done so is another of the tragic follies by which Christians down the centuries have frustrated the will of the Great Commission himself.

But the memory of the Lord's prayer for unity has never quite been lost, even when, in pursuit of it, men thought that unity must mean uniformity. It was the grim and bloody breaking of the medieval dream of unity in the sixteenth century which began to drive some Christians to see if they could find a unity which could include differences. The story of this search has been finely told in a book edited by Ruth Rouse and Stephen Neill, *A History of the Ecumenical Movement, 1517-1948.*

A point of incalculable importance must be noted. As the Lord's prayer for unity came to grip men's imagination, so they were driven to pray for unity themselves. Two little-remembered dates are important. In 1819 the Secretaries of the London-based missionary societies began the practice of a monthly meeting for prayer about their work. In 1825 the Bombay Missionary Union was formed bringing together Anglican, Brethren, Congregational and Presbyterian missionaries to pray together and discuss together how to find areas of agreement and so avoid friction. From this local initiative the principle of 'comity' came to be worked out whereby Missions who were willing to co-operate agreed to demarcate their areas of work and so avoid overlapping. In an age of relative immobility this worked reasonably well. Problems arose when Christians of one tradition moved into an area 'occupied' by those of another tradition. However, the attempt proved an incentive towards closer unity. Unfortunately, it has to be recorded that Roman Catholic Missions refused to observe any such principle. We had to wait for Pope John XXIII before, in dramatic fashion, this iceberg of disunity began to melt.

This nineteenth century missionary initiative saw its climax in the great Missionary Conference at Edinburgh in 1910, significant, not so much for anything said, as for one decision made, namely that a continuation committee be formed to go on exploring further the unity already achieved. This continuation committee became the International Missionary Council. An American, Bishop Brent of the Philippines, saw another need and persevered to establish another ecumenical committee to be concerned with 'Faith and Order', thus discovering what were the theological obstacles to unity. Later, the Swedish Bishop Söderblom took the initiative in starting what came to be called the committee for 'Life and Work' aiming to see what were the implications of the Christian Faith for the social, economic and political order.

In all this enterprise one great weakness remained. The voices that were heard were almost exclusively from the western world. The Churches of what, today, we call the 'Third World', were voiceless. Not surprisingly that voice began to be heard from India. On May 1-2, 1919, a Conference, under the Chairmanship of an Indian, Bishop Azariah, and consisting, with two exceptions, entirely of Indians, met at Tranquebar in South India. In 1947, the hopes there expressed achieved concrete form in the Church of South India, in which Anglicans, Congregationalists, Methodists and Presbyterians, jointly took the risk of spiritual enrichment. The full and fascinating story can be read in *Church of South India — The Movement Towards Union, 1900-1947*, by Bishop Bengt Sundkler.

All this ecumenical ferment reached a new point of achievement when, in 1948 at Amsterdam, the World Council of Churches came into being, emphatically not as a super-Church but as the forum in which the responsible representatives of the Churches could wrestle together over common problems, and serve as a pressure group within each particular Church, asking awkward questions about the meaning of unity. In 1961 at the World Council Assembly in New Delhi the Orthodox Churches of Russia, Romania, Bulgaria and Poland were welcomed as members. The Church of Rome still hesitates. History is still too strong, but official observers were already present at New Delhi. In innumerable ways the initiatives of Pope John XXIII are being followed up.

At that same New Delhi Conference the International Missionary Council, the main instrument hitherto for fostering co-operation in evangelism, was integrated with the World

Council of Churches, the great hope being that this would inject
an evangelistic urgency into an organisation which seemed
over-preoccupied with ecclesiastical structures. A valuable
book by Norman Goodall *Ecumenical Progress — A Decade of
Change in the Ecumenical Movement 1961-1971* brings the story
nearer to our own day. But a large question mark about
evangelism remains.

The church in the 'Third World'

A significant fact about this period is that, by its end, the
Churches of the 'Third World', the fruit of the foreign
missionary movement, had become self-governing. Nationalist
sentiment, apart from theological considerations, made this as
imperative as it was timely. But the economic factor has
prevented these Churches achieving full financial independence. This still poses great problems, as does the contribution
of man-power from the economically more prosperous nations.
Amour propre and realism do not always come up with the
same answers to these problems. Independence does not, of
itself, ensure that a Church will be fired with the urgency of the
great commission.

Nevertheless, in many places there is an upsurge of evangelistic zeal. This, of course, was never a monopoly of the western
missionary. But, today, more than ever before in many parts of
Africa, Asia and Latin America the pioneer thrust of the
evangelist is being made by their own sons and daughters. This
gives a new dimension to William Temple's 'Great new fact of
our era'.

Protest movements

Another phenomenon of these years has to be taken very
seriously. Independent Church movements have proliferated in
Africa and are present in Asia. In some measure they are an
indigenous protest against the indigestible western accessories
to the Faith purveyed by the western Churches through their
missionaries. These Churches are growing very rapidly in
Africa and may well have a determining influence on the future
shape of African Christianity.

Another movement, substantially of this century and growing in influence during these sixty years, has been the
movement of Pentecostalism. Essentially it is a protest movement in the positive sense of insisting that Christians must take
the empowering and guidance of the Holy Spirit much more
seriously in their individual lives and in their corporate
activities, than is commonly the case.

An overflow from this movement is the Charismatic movement as it is being experienced in all the more traditional
Churches, not least in the Roman Catholic Church. Seeking to
remain an integral part of these Churches, the Charismatic
movement is a serious attempt to help Christians to receive
from the Holy Spirit that newness of life to which so much
conventional Christianity has been blind.

All these three manifestations of revolt against the conventional and the comfortable, and the tyranny of the accidental,
cannot easily be assessed as to their enduring importance.
What at least can be said is that their enthusiasm and devotion
are healthy corrections to the torpidity of so much church life.
Their missionary potential is incalculable.

No serious interpretation of the years 1909-69 can avoid
facing the fact that, during these years, there has been in the
West an ebb-tide of Christian faith, and of Christian practice
in the sphere of public worship, and of moral standards. It is
none-the-less facile and extremely dangerous to use the cliché
'a post-Christian world' as a description of the western scene.
If that term means anything it implies a post-Christ world,
which for a Christian ought to be recognised as blasphemy.

It is worth remembering that no sixty years in all history
since the Crucifixion have seen so many men and women being
martyred because of their faith in the Crucified. The martyrdom has often meant not only death, but the living experience
of persecution and discrimination because of faith. There is
nothing post-Christian in that record. Have we any reason
whatever for believing that the blood of these martyrs is unable
to produce a harvest? The blood-groups have not changed.

Nor is there any justification for despair lest Christians today
will not be able to out-think their contemporaries as they did in

earlier times. Sustained and self-critical thinking about the Christian Faith has blossomed as in no previous century. It has today no parallel, either in secular-humanist circles, or in the other great religions of mankind. And there is an openness to new understanding of the Faith and of other Faiths, and a new approach to un-faith, which is one of the most exciting evidences of Christian vitality.

To explore the implications of this will be the task of Part III. This chapter has been written with the conviction that an awareness of the most significant developments of these sixty years is essential if we are to spell out the meaning of the great commission for today and for the tomorrow which will so soon be today.

PART III

What Spelling it Out Means Today

The secular society, unrestrained by a religious outlook, moves inexorably towards diabolical tyranny. The individualistic society in which enlightened self-interest takes the place of *agape* degenerates rapidly into chaos and gives way to the same tyranny in the end. The Church which seeks to impose objective sanctions to enforce theological truth or to enact rigid objective codes of practical conduct in the end finds itself deserted by its adherents. But a body of these, returning always to the source of their inspiration, and making use of the covenanted means of grace, always survives to renew the life of the new Israel. This life manifests itself in the inner light vouchsafed to the individual. But it protects itself in little circles of human beings attempting, however unsuccessfully, to develop the kingdom by practising *agape* towards one another and moving outwards into the hostile secular environment in which they are placed to gain new adherents and to do good even to those who persecute it and hate it.

Lord Hailsham
The Door Wherein I Went

CHAPTER 6

Reviewing the Present

ON THE FIFTH Sunday after Easter in the year 1933 a sermon
was preached from the pulpit of the church in Berlin-Dahlem.
I quote —

> The Lord Jesus Christ has founded His community and set
> it in the midst of the nations — in our nation as well — so
> that it may proclaim Him as the one and only Mediator, so
> that any man who inquires after God — so that any nation
> which begins to seek God — may meet Him, the Christ of
> God, and not pass Him by.
>
> The result of this meeting does not lie within our power;
> but it is incumbent upon us to see that it takes place, and
> that it takes place in such a way that the holy and gracious
> will of God is revealed: "God will have all men to be saved
> and to come to the knowledge of the truth!" If today there is
> an inquiring and a seeking after God — and there is: we can
> all hear and see it for ourselves — then God is seeking us
> and asking us what message we are proclaiming; then he
> wishes us to testify concerning the Lord Jesus Christ so
> loudly, so clearly and so plainly that all this inquiring and
> seeking must explain itself to Him and must render an
> account of itself to Him.*

That was bravely said. And Dr. Martin Niemöller who said it

---

*This quotation and the one at the end of Chapter 10 will be found in
a book by Dr Martin Niemöller with the title *First Commandment*,
published in 1937 by William Hodge & Co, London.

was a very brave man indeed. He was speaking to a congregation in a Germany in which Hitler had just come to power.
Those who know his story know the price he paid for his
courageous ministry. But I quote that passage here out of
context. I quote it as a fine statement which would be relevant
at any moment in history, anywhere, and never more relevant
than when the reader reaches this page.

The 'how' of testimony

The question which the reader must now ask himself is
'How is this proclamation to be made?' No-one can doubt that
in our world there is much 'inquiring and seeking after God',
even when the word 'God' is only confusedly understood, or
even mistakenly repudiated. The world, consciously or unconsciously, is looking for salvation. How, then, do we imagine we
can, to quote Dr. Niemöller, 'testify concerning the Lord Jesus
Christ so loudly, so clearly and so plainly that all this inquiring
and seeking must explain itself to Him?'

Obviously there is no easy answer. We, as members of the
community of Christ, are ourselves part of the reason why the
answer is so difficult. By this I do not simply mean our own
manifest failure as Christians to obey the great commission. I
mean that we are the heirs to centuries of failure, even when
we are also heirs to the problems of success.

In Part II I attempted a kaleidoscope of nineteen centuries
of history, bright with heroic endeavour, yes, but also dark
with much failure and tragedy. We are the heirs of that history.
Deliberately I played down the measure of success — the fact
that the community of Christ is now world-wide is some
measure of the obedience attempted — and rather stressed the
ambiguous legacy of success. It is the ambiguity of that success
which is one of our major problems.

As I have insisted, in obeying the great commission, we
Christians have been part of history. We cannot escape that
fact, nor ought we to wish to do so. In our enthusiasm for Mission we need to be kept very humble. There has been so much
failure. The Jew, the Muslim and the Communist are witnesses
to that. Nor can we escape from the very fact that the Church,
as world-wide, owes much to its links with commercial,

cultural, and political colonialism. In the long perspectives of future history, if such there is to be, men may be a little less emotionally excited by the word 'colonialism' than they are today. But it is today for which we are responsible.

Other men's shoes

Now, as I said earlier, I have written this book from the standpoint of a Christian of the West. I could do no other, for such I am. But all the while I have been trying to put myself in other men's shoes — those of our fellow Christians of Asia and Africa and Latin America, as well as those of men of other Faiths or none. I have tried to think what they have been thinking as they read that history, as they have experienced that history. And, as I have tried to do this, I have had to ask myself 'What have they really heard?' It is no use our speaking 'so loudly' and, so we imagine, 'so clearly and plainly' when, in fact, they are not at all hearing what we are saying, because they are thinking differently. This, as we shall see later, has its own direct bearing on the language we use, on our knowledge of their language. We have, indeed, like the prophet of the Exile, to begin by sitting where they sit (Ezek. 3:15). It is likely to prove as overwhelming an experience for us as it was for him. And because this commission is so very difficult we may find ourselves sharing some of the prophet's 'bitterness of spirit'. It is all so very unlike our traditional picture of the missionary work of the Church!

Our 'thought's wildernesses'

Am I so very wrong in thinking that much of the despondency and defeatism of so many Christians about Mission in any form, even when they are deeply concerned about the great commission and obedience to it, derives from this overwhelming perplexity of how to set about it?

Certainly there is much to daunt us Christians of the West. There was a time when, with some measure of truth, we could maintain that a civilisation had emerged in the West which possessed some moral values to which those of other civilisations might accord some respect. Indeed those values did gain such respect in considerable measure. But it was not because they were our values. Rather it was because something of the light of the gospel had filtered through them. Other men's values responded to what they felt was valuable in ours. In spite of our Western trappings the seed of the gospel often fell into fertile soil.

But two world-wars initiated by the West have changed all that: our general surrender to a crude materialism: the proved fact that only the painful experience of our own standards of living being under threat from the Third World has made us take that Third World at all seriously: it is these things that have stultified the moral appeal of the West. That is one very big reason why so much 'inquiring and seeking' today is not directed towards a Faith so closely identified with a West in such total social, moral, and political, not to mention economic, disarray. No wonder so many peoples in the world, and not least so many in the West, are seeking light from the East.

But we must press the difficulty of our being obedient to the great commission a little further. We saw, in the last chapter of Part II, how the Frankenstein of industrial and commercial complexity — of multiple interdependence — seems to dwarf the possibility of any worthwhile individual initiative.

Meanwhile, our crude materialism — get rich quickly at any price — has spawned a twin Frankenstein, the fouling of our environment. There is something here far more deep-seated than the carelessness of allowing chemical effluents to pour into our rivers and into the sea. It is, in the long run, even more serious than the disposal of atomic waste. These are really just the more ugly symptoms of a sickness in the soul of man. We see the same thing in the kind of building development which creates concrete jungles. It shows itself in a total indifference to nature whether in its fauna or flora. It is found wherever we find the fundamental stupidity which sacrifices beauty to material gain, killing whales, for instance, to provide cosmetics! Dare we add the subtlest pollution of all, the degradation, the fouling of language? I do not mean four-letter words. The illiterate and the inarticulate have always used them. We foul our language most when we torture the meaning of words to fit a headline or produce a snappy advertisement. 'Crisis', for instance, is a very great word indeed. Properly used, it means an occasion when an individual, a group, or a nation face some test which brings them and their values and their practice — their faith — under judgment. Crises in history have been some of the great occasions in which men have discovered God. Read the Old Testament prophets if you doubt that, and note that the God they discovered was as uncomfortable as he was true. What have we done with the word 'crisis'? Thanks to the Media it can now mean anything or nothing. The one thing it never means now is a revelation of God. We cannot afford to lose the moments of revelation. We cannot afford the fouling of our language.

In reviewing the present there is material enough for gloom, for pessimism, for hopelessness. But rose-coloured spectacles are bad for the eyes of the mind. The factors in our present which have been highlighted here have been so exposed of purpose because, in the deep recesses of our souls, they raise the queries which paralyse. In quite another sense than Shelley's these queries haunt our 'thought's wildernesses'. With Hamlet we know all too well how 'enterprises of great pith and moment' can 'lose the name of action.' So let us bring all this out into the open. By refusing to face unpleasant and disconcerting facts, by being unwilling to understand them, by being deaf to what God is saying out of the midst of them, too many Christians who know quite well that the great commission has not been countermanded, find their nerves in tatters.

CHAPTER 7

The Recovery of Nerve

IF WE WHO believe in the Great Commission himself; if we wish to obey what he has committed to us; if we would have our tattered nerves restored to their proper functions of fitting us for high endeavour; if we would embark on new voyages of exploration, and make unexpected discoveries; there is a first step which we must take. We must recover our faith that God is in control of history, with the corollary that the God who is in control of history is himself uncontrollable.

God the uncontrollable

One of the most creative moments in man's spiritual pilgrimage was when the great prophets of Israel became aware that God was uncontrollable precisely because he was really in control. The Hebrew people had settled themselves comfortably with the illusion that, because they were a chosen people, it was up to God to look after his choice. They, the people of the Covenant, the people of privilege, could live in safety, certainty and enjoyment, whatever happened around them. Because of the Covenant they thought they had a measure of control over history because of their control over God. It was in order to awake their people from this illusion that the great prophets broke silence.

'You only have I known of all the families of the earth: therefore I will punish you for all your iniquities' (Amos 3:2 A.V.). Read the devastating sixth chapter of the same prophet, where he asks in what respect were the Covenant people better than their neighbours. Hear the final shattering of all complacency — 'Did I not bring Israel up from Egypt, the Philistines from Capthor, the Arameans from Kir?' (9:7). Philistines and Arameans, too, were chosen for some pupose. God is the God of history. God is in control. Perish illusion!

Isaiah lived through the aftermath of one of the greatest reigns in his people's history, that of Uzziah. Painfully he came to the conclusion that both he and his people had presumed on their privileged position, and now the Assyrian was at the gate. Read, in chapter six, his tremendous experience of seeing 'the Lord seated on a throne, high and exalted', obviously in control of events. Then read his commission to the chosen people who thought that being chosen gave them an historical immunity from trouble.

Again, feel the poignant agony of Jeremiah, who, in the last days of the Hebrew kingship, struggled at infinite cost to himself to preach political sanity, and failed to carry conviction. He was to have a vision of a new covenant, very different from the one his people cherished, and, in hope, believed against hope, a hope not to be realised for more than six hundred years.

No, there was little joy in being a prophet who insisted that God the uncontrollable was in control. What a tremendous experience came to the prophet Habakkuk. A careful student of political events, baffled at the prospect of the impending destruction of the Covenant people at the hands of a brutal enemy, he heard a staggering word from God, 'I am raising up the Chaldeans, that savage and impetuous nation' (1:6).

It has been wisely said that 'there is nothing so frightening to man as an uncontrollable God'. That is why, in the long history of man, all his religions have made systematic attempts to bring God under, at least, some measure of control. Even our Christian theologies have tried to prescribe his possibilities. Consider the elaborate efforts to confine the activities of the Holy Spirit to certain specific means of grace. How much genuine social, political and economic content have we Christians given to the words, so often on our lips, 'Thy will be done on earth as it is in heaven'? Do we Christians of the New Covenant really imagine that, like the people of the Old Covenant, we can leave the doing of God's will to God, while we enjoy our privileges undisturbed?

These questions must be asked and answered if we are to be

taken seriously in our belief that God is in control of history, and
that his will is to be done *in* history. But it must be his will, not
ours. We cannot manipulate him to suit our convenience.

On reading the signs of the times

There is a passage of very great interest in Luke 11:29-32
where Jesus is seen surrounded by an eager crowd demanding
some evidence of God's activity in their situation. Jesus refers
them back to their history. They are bidden to remember the
story of Solomon and the Queen of Sheba, and the story of
Nineveh and the prophet Jonah. Now, on the strength of that
passage in Luke, the translators of the Authorised Version would
seem to be fully justified, against the evidence of some manu-
scripts, in inserting what Jesus said to some of the Pharisees and
Sadducees who were in the crowd — 'O ye hypocrites, ye can
discern the face of the sky; but can ye not discern the signs of the
times?' (Matt. 16:3 A.V.). Jesus was making an appeal to
contemporary history. Jesus himself was a sign, a prophetic sign.

The whole challenge of the ministry of Jesus was in line
with that of the great prophets of the Old Testament in their
witness to the rule of God, and the demands of his righteousness. The ethics of Jesus were not just personal, designed for
individuals. They had social and political implications. As a
matter of history he died as a social and political subversive.
That fact of history has its own significance for history, then
and now. As Christians we are sure that the Cross had a
meaning not limited to history, that 'God was in Christ
reconciling the world to himself' (2 Cor. 5:19) in ways which
altogether transcend history. Yet that reconciliation was also
taking place in history. Caiaphas and Pilate thought they were
in control. But they were no more in control of events than had
been Cyrus the Persian. In Isaiah 45:4-7 we overhear, through
the prophet, God saying to Cyrus, 'I have called you by name
and given you your title, though you have not known me... I
will strengthen you though you have not known me... I am the
Lord, there is no other; I make the light, I create darkness,
author alike of prosperity and trouble. I, the Lord, do all these
things.' That is a very pregnant passage about the uncontrollable God, who is in control of history.

I have dwelt at this length on the witness of Scripture to the relationship of God to history, in part to give a true perspective. I hope what I have written may encourage some to receive the same therapy which was provided for Amos and Isaiah, for Jeremiah and Habakkuk, and which is part of the wonder of the Event which is Jesus Christ.

My other reason for this Scriptural introduction is to insist that we today are to be on the alert for the signs of God's working in our history, not just in the past, but in the present, with an eye alert to God's future. I believe that we can mark his footsteps, almost hear them, if we look around us and listen. Remembering that Cyrus did not *know* that he was in God's service, let us look at some of the signs of our times, and be not faithless but believing. For this purpose I list *seven* signs of the times.

(1) The compassionate society

First, there is the fact of what may properly be called 'the Compassionate Society'. At times we are, indeed, almost overwhelmed by the violence of our times. We see on T.V., almost while it is happening, the devastating effects of a typhoon in Bangladesh or Darwin: the appalling tragedy of an earthquake in Turkey. Even more shattering still is the grim inhumanity of man to man which is the staple theme of all the Media. We watched Vietnam with horror. Then came Chile. At the time of writing (January 1976) it is Angola and the Lebanon. Who knows where it will be next? Who knows what is happening now behind closed frontiers, and with a censored press?

Yet, it is within this world of so much suffering and violence that we are seeing the birth of a compassionate society, such as the world has never seen before. Any great physical disaster calls out immediate compassionate aid from all over the world. Do we give adequate interpretation to the tremendous canalisation of the ordinary person's compassion through Christian Aid, through Tear Fund, through Oxfam, to think of Britain alone? Have we assessed adequately the enormous contribution made by American men and women to Church World Service, and to every effort which affords an outlet to compassion for human need? Are we aware of the vast contributions made by

voluntary agencies in Germany, Scandinavia and the Nether-
lands to help the under-privileged of the Third World? These
are only illustrations of what ordinary people are doing, with
no political or economic or religious strings attached. Governments make loans which, of course, add to the indebtedness of
the recipients, or are just blatantly bilateral in their operation.
Not so the ordinary men and women who are creating the
compassionate society.

What does all this mean? No claim is being made here for
Christian philanthropy. Many who are contributing to this
compassion are not consciously responding to Jesus Christ.
The movement is much wider. Something new is happening.
Can we hear the footsteps of him who once told the story of the
final judgment upon man at the end of man's history, which we
find in Matthew 25:31-46?

(2) The passion for justice

Second, there is as one world-wide phenomenon of our time
the passion for justice. Was there ever a time when that passion
was blazing, so like a forest-fire as it is today?

This passion for justice takes many forms. In one place and
another it will be a protest against discrimination on grounds of
colour. At least one continent, Africa, is convulsed by this
injustice. And the convulsion, as we know, has spilled over, far
outside Africa. In Latin America, on the other hand, the revolt
is against political, economic, and social injustice, gross and
merciless exploitation of the poor. In Asia the picture is
different again. Generalisation is impossible. But common to
every country in Asia is revolt against exploitation by foreigners. In one form or another, in a degree never known
before, there is in every country a rising tide of demand for
justice. Much of the world's violence is an expression of this
demand. In Britain, and in many other western countries, a
concern about real justice is the leit-motif of all politics,
whatever their complexion.

In one specialist field, Amnesty International expresses the
conscience of mankind, and is addressed indiscriminately to
wherever there are prisoners of conscience, or men and women
are imprisoned without trial.

Again, if we white-skinned peoples of the West did not get into such an emotional brain-storm at the mention of Communism, we might remember what an ancient idea it is. It has taken many forms, not the least significant having been Buddhist and Christian monasticism. We too easily forget that the most modern articulation of the Communist ideal came as a fiery protest against the horrors of the nineteenth century industrial scene. We are fully entitled to our belief that the particular development of Marxism which could produce Stalin was a deviation which, in the name of that very justice which Karl Marx demanded, must be resisted if any kind of civilisation is to survive. But let us ask ourselves candidly how far we are altogether satisfied that, west of the Iron curtain, our social and economic expression of justice has a wholly 'acceptable face'.

How much have we troubled to discover what Marxists are thinking? How aware are we that the very phenomenon of Stalin and Stalinism is actually provoking a great debate within the Marxist world itself? God is just as capable today as he was in 538 B.C. (Cyrus) of using some very strange historical developments to achieve his purpose. Let us watch, without being frightened at what is happening. Let us listen without having heart in mouth. There are some unexpected footmarks in our world. There is a sound of hurrying feet.

If you want the standard work on justice you will find it in the Old Testament.

(3) The search for meaning

A *third* sign of the times is the search for meaning. Who am I? Here, in that very question, is perhaps the point at which the generation gap is most acutely felt. The older generation, to which the writer belongs, either found the answer long ago, or have given up the search. But the search is a very lively affair in the younger generation. They are asking the question with passion. They are rarely willing to accept any definition provided by tradition, least of all if suggested by that older generation, which they feel to be responsible for the mess in which they find themselves.

Nor are these young limited to the youth of the West.

Wherever traditions have been abandoned; wherever the old fabric of society is being progressively destroyed; in refugee camps in the Middle East; among the vast army of unemployed graduates in India; among Asian immigrant communities in Europe; wherever the devastation of war has broken up family and social life; there the question is being asked — 'Who am I?'

It is another universal phenomenon that, in their search for meaning, the young of all the world feel themselves to be far more akin with those of their own generation, without regard to race, than they do with their own older generation.

The cynic may say that long before Shakespeare's 'sixth age shifts into the lean and slipper'd pantaloon, with spectacles on nose', the young will have come to terms with reality, and will cease to be curious as to who they are. They will have become, so the cynic avers, far too busy to ask questions. But is the cynic right? There is much to suggest that this radical questioning has come to stay for quite a long time. The perspective of mankind about the universe has changed out of all recognition in this century. The very survival of the human race introduces today a new depth to the questioning. Science, philosophy and religion are all conspiring to press the question 'What is man?' The young only simplify the issue by personalising it, 'Who am I?' This fundamental search for meaning is a sign of our time.

(4) Interiorisation

A *fourth* sign of the times, not without some links with the third, I would define as the phenomenon of 'interiorisation'. This is, in essence, a protest against the pressures of our mass society. It could be described as a form of prayer, an inward wrestling, a fighting refusal to accept defeat by acquiescing in the 'bread and circuses' offered by society as an anodyne. From such praying, once become corporate, develops the life-style of a homogeneous group. Some of the kibbutzim in Israel take this form; as once did the Jesus colonies in China; as ashrams have done in the age-old tradition of India. They are often called communes, though, once again, there is nothing new about this.

What is new is the scale and range of such experiments. Indeed, what we are seeing is a movement which corresponds in many particulars with what, in the fourth and fifth centuries, has been called the 'flight to the desert'. At the heart of that so-called flight was a protest against current conventional values, a hunger for the eternal and the enduring. What is more, it was a very profound way of praying, with a life-style to match. Before we lightly dismiss that ancient protest, or its latest manifestations, as attempted escapes from the world, we do well to remember that from that earlier 'withdrawal' there was, in Toynbee's phrase, a very dramatic 'return'. An impulse from the desert fathers gripped the imagination of Benedict of Nursia, the founder of western monasticism, to which spiritual enterprise European medieval civilisation owed its soul. It could happen again.

Interiorisation — the grappling of the individual with the angel in his own soul — what H.E. Fosdick, long ago, called 'the prayer of dominant desire', can lead to *exteriorisation* in most dramatic ways. The great religious revivals of recent centuries, to go no further back, all began with the prayer-battle in some individual life. The resulting spiritual renewal was communicated to a wider group, and then out to society.

This fourth sign could prove to be the most important of all the signs of the times — the hearing once again of the 'still small voice' (1 Kings 19:12 A.V.).

(5) The search for belonging

This search, our *fifth* sign, can be distinguished under many very different forms. It is to be found, for instance, wherever the cataclysmic forces of change compel men to be members of two worlds, at home in neither. To be socially uprooted from a stable world of custom and habit is to feel an almost passionate desire to 'belong' somewhere, somehow. Apart from the obvious trauma for members of a primitive culture finding themselves in a world of modern technology, there is the much more widespread trauma for the peasant finding himself an urban-dweller. These are the tragic commonplaces of our time.

In particular, the traditional Christian Churches are discovering painfully what the ebb-tide of faith means in practice.

In much of the Western world, but not only there, multitudes of 'church-goers' have voted with their feet. For one reason or another they do not 'belong' any more. But they *must* 'belong' somewhere and so find substitute 'homes' — mostly with a minimum religious content.

These same traditional Churches are having to face the fact that the fastest growing Churches today are Pentecostal Churches and, in Africa, and to some extent in Asia, what are known as Independent Churches. These all have an intense corporate life. In them the fellowship of the Holy Spirit is experienced as a warm pulsating reality. You know you 'belong'. In the case of the Independent Churches of Africa there is the distinguishing characteristic that they are trying to graft Christian insights on to the traditional cultures of Africa. Here for many Africans is a spiritual home where he feels he can 'belong'.

This, of course, is to over-simplify a complicated issue. But, however the more traditional Churches interpret this sign, it is one which has to be taken seriously. Do the hurrying feet of so many into these new Christian shapes, or into 'homes' with no Christian form at all, suggest that Someone's footfall is hurrying after? That question must be pressed. The charismatic movement which is now being found in all the Churches, even the most traditional, is part of the pressure.

(6) The search for unity

The *sixth* sign is man's search for unity. Science is demonstrating that this is one world. Scientists are among the pioneers in the effort to establish the unity of mankind. They already constitute an impressive international community of their own. And within this international community of science it is becoming commonplace to recognise that co-operative endeavour makes nonsense of any exclusive claim by one individual to be a 'discoverer'. Discovery is team work and it is international team work.

There is one very important by-product of this world-view of science in what is happening to man's awareness of himself in history. Professor Jürgen Moltmann has put it like this—

Nowhere on earth is the future any longer simply a

continuation of the past; today for every nation it is something new. There was in fact no 'world history' before. There were only the histories of various peoples and cultures in their separate worlds. Only now are we entering a future in which we will be able to talk about one world history. In the past, men had histories only in the plural. Therefore our pasts are plural today. Every people, every culture, every religion has its own history and its particular traditions. Because from now on we will either be destroyed together or survive in a new community, our future is only singular.

We are moving forward into unity, however halting our progress, however fiercely we continue to hug the past. Tragically, for the most part, we lack the vision of the Seer of the Book of Revelation who could look forward to a future city into which the wealth and splendour of every nation's history would be brought (Rev. 21:26). The point that needs making here is that at last we can share his prophetic perspective because we can see that history is moving in this direction.

Who is the source of all man's wisdom? Who is the Lord of history? As Christians we believe we have the answer. We believe that even if mankind's drive towards unity were to be so tainted by evil as to point only to the unity of hell, yet God's redemptive purpose would prevail. And it is with that redemptive purpose that our great commission is concerned.

(7) The ecumenical movement

I make bold to suggest that the *seventh* sign is the ecumenical movement. This movement takes many forms. But it is a spirit long before it takes any institutional form. What is more, it has many institutional forms, whether local or global. Understood in this sense, the ecumenical movement is part of the answer to our Lord's High Priestly Prayer, as we have it presented in the seventeenth chapter of John's Gospel. We must assume that our Lord has been praying that prayer ever since, that he is still praying it, and that his Spirit is articulating our longings (Rom. 8:26), so as to identify them with the heavenly intercession of our Lord himself.

We will each of us have our own special experience of ecumenicity. But do not let us ever sin against the unity of the Spirit by despising, or lightly dismissing the experience of ecumenicity which others enjoy.

I have before me, as I write, a formidable document — *Report on Nuclear Energy* — dated October 1975. It is a Report to the Churches, produced under the auspices of the World Council of Churches. The greater part of the document is far beyond my understanding. But I can understand the last chapter on 'Ethical reflections on the use of Nuclear Energy'. Here I find myself very much at home, either as a prospective victim, or as a prospective beneficiary. What I would note here is that there is no other Christian agency in existence, other than the World Council of Churches, capable of sponsoring such a Report.

Whatever our views of the World Council of Churches, whatever our ecumenical criticisms of it may be, let us try to get things in proportion. From the Media and, in particular, the correspondence in the Church press, from time to time, it could be imagined that the energies of the World Council of Churches are exclusively directed to politics. This, of course, is untrue, though politics inescapably have their place. What cannot be stressed too often is that the main concern of the World Council of Churches is to provide a forum where Christians, of many traditions and very varying pasts, are trying to learn with each other to think about that 'singular future' in which we are all involved.

The World Council of Churches is, on any reckoning, *one* important symbol of man's search for unity, a search specifically promoted by men and women who are seeking the mind of Christ as to the unity which he wants for the Church. The great commission involves far more than the pursuit of Christian unity, but it certainly includes it.

In listing these seven signs I make no dogmatic claim about their actual or relative significance. Rather, I offer them as signs 'positive' in a time of so many 'negative', world-denying, God-denying signs. As such, they are, at least, suggestive of possibilities. Matthew's Gospel, in the passage already quoted, also tells us that the Pharisees and Sadducees were quite good as weather prophets. What Jesus regretted was their inability to look any further. So, believing as I do that God is in control of history, I look for signs of his activity in our times. What this chapter has attempted has been the simple task of presenting certain encouraging factors which are part of the setting within which the great commission has to be obeyed today.

The setting of the first attempt at obedience was the precarious world of the Roman Empire. Then came the attempt made within the geographically circumscribed limits of medieval Europe, not forgetting the heroic attempts towards China and India and the Nile valley. The next attempt at obedience coincided with the expansion of Europe from the fifteenth to the twentieth century. This was followed by the age of technology in which, of course, we are still living. In each of these past ages the strategy and tactics of the Christian attempt to obey the great commission were largely determined by a particular history.

Now we are in a new order, a new history. We must assume that our strategy and our tactics will, in some respects, be very different from those of the past. The commission remains. Our duty is faithfulness. I do not forget the conviction from which I started that God is uncontrollable. What he may do in our present history, only God knows.

CHAPTER 8

Religious Pluralism

THE SENSE IN which religious pluralism is to be understood here and in the following chapters calls for some definition. Here, it will be understood as one aspect of that global village which is our world. It will be concerned with the interactions of cultures which are intermingling today with an intensity never known before. We will have to ask what it means in very practical terms in Rotterdam, the Ruhr, Marseilles, Birmingham, Bradford and Southall, and in countless other places in Europe. For here it is a new problem. In great seaports there have always been small enclaves of Muslims and Hindus. But it is a new experience in Europe to have some schools in which fifty per cent or more of the children are Hindus or Muslims.

Religious pluralism, however, must be seen as a much wider problem than something being experienced in Europe. The Middle East has known it for centuries, and not only since 1948. There, for centuries it was dealt with by comprehensive legislation. Christians, Jews and Muslims lived together, if not easily, at least for the most part in peace. The confusion in the Middle East today is essentially political and not religious in character.

In Africa, religious pluralism takes various forms, from the commonplace of Yoruba life in Nigeria where an extended family may have Christian, Muslim and Pagan members sharing the same compound, to an effective apartheid in Southern Africa. This latter, however, is primarily cultural and not religious.

How in fact are we to distinguish culture and religion? In any given culture there can be religious pluralism within a broad religious consensus, as has been manifestly the case with Christianity, Hinduism, Islam, and Buddhism.

One of the most successful examples of both religious and cultural pluralism, so far achieved, has been Hawaii where, to an extraordinary degree, harmonious relations have been established between Polynesians, Asians and Caucasians. Again, that vast melting-pot of cultures, the U.S.A., presents its own pattern, quite unlike anything else attempted in the world. Its great achievements are too easily forgotten in the social, political and economic convulsions of a great nation suddenly confronting a wholly new range of challenges to its very existence. Martin Luther King is a better guide through that labyrinth than Malcolm X, though Malcolm X needs more sympathetic understanding than he has always received.

Obviously, we are dealing here with an immensely complicated issue. Perhaps it will clarify things a little if we deliberately look upon it first as a global issue, as being intimately involved in what, in the previous chapter, we saw as one of the signs of the times — the pursuit of unity. Is it possible that we are meant to see religious pluralism itself as a sign, and, as in the case of the other signs, as carrying within it the footmarks of the God of history?

At first sight, the sudden juxtaposition of cultures at the local level, profoundly shaped as they are by religious assumptions, makes for tension and conflict, and certainly does not contribute to peace and unity. Rather, at the local level, such juxtaposition creates fear. A previously assumed cultural unity, whether religiously felt or not, considers itself threatened by something alien. This is the common reaction at the local level. Religious pluralism, viewed as cultural pluralism, is resented and resisted. When, to every other factor, there is added a time of economic distress and the threat of unemployment, tension can lead to violence, and does.

There is then a local situation and a global situation. Let us be frank and admit that for most people if they attempt to read the signs of the times, and I am thinking of Christians, it will be easier to recognise a sign in the global situation, which remains conveniently remote, than in the local situation where, as citizens in a multi-racial community, they are more personally involved.

A global conversation

The global situation, first created by the expansion of Europe, and now dramatically experienced through every form of communication, and by technology, means that increasing numbers of people are crossing old cultural barriers. We are being compelled to think globally, and we find ourselves in a global conversation in which Atheists, Buddhists, Christians, Hindus, Jews and Muslims, not to mention the devotees of the syncretistic new religions of Japan, and of what Lanternari has called 'the Religions of the Oppressed', are all talking together.

This is something quite new. As yet it has hardly begun to impinge on the man in the pew, and, so far, appears to have had little more impact on the man in the pulpit, or, with a few exceptions, the professor in his Chair. I speak of the Britain I know. How far things are better or worse elsewhere I do not presume to guess.

What must surely be obvious is that Christians, as Christians, must think very seriously about the meaning of this global conversation. Is it to be viewed as a tremendous threat to the Christian gospel, a sign of 'the last times' when a cold breath of agnosticism and relativism ensures that, when the Son of Man comes, he will find no faith on the earth? There are certainly Christians who think like this. Are they right?

But if such despair is resisted, as, I believe, it must be resisted, then perhaps this conversation is to be welcomed. That could, however, let us face it, be a very facile conclusion, and the temptation to be facile is very much with us. Reacting, and reacting rightly, against the dogmatic triumphalism of much past Christian approach to men of other Faiths, it is all too easy to swing to the other extreme and talk happily of different roads to the summit, as if Jesus were in no particular and distinctive sense 'the Way, the Truth, and the Life'. Of course, where this point is reached, the great commission is tacitly, if not explicitly, held to be indefinitely in suspense, if not quite otiose. This is a view forcefully propounded by some Christians holding professorial Chairs in Britain and across the Atlantic. Are they right? Is courtesy always to preclude contradiction? Is choice now just a matter of taste, no longer a response to an absolute demand? Is the Cross on Calvary really no more than a confusing roundabout sign pointing in every direction, or is it still the place where *all* men are meant to kneel?

I believe that we are called to welcome this conversation, without reservations, but not as a place of easy accommodation and polite evasion. Rather we are to see it as the opportunity where we may expect to discover a Jesus *incognito*. At the same time, we will be no less ready, expectantly, ourselves to uncover the Christ of our experience. Those who have joined in such conversations can testify that Jesus is never shouted down. For our part, then, as we join the conversations we are to hold ourselves ready. The Son of Man may come at a time and in a manner which will take everyone by surprise. There is plenty of Scripture to support that conviction. So let us welcome the wonderful new opportunities for conversation provided by the global fact of religious pluralism.

A local conversation

For most Christians this welcome will necessarily be experienced as an attitude of mind, all the more important for being an attitude devoid of fear. But it will remain at the level of attitude having only rare opportunities for expression. Quite otherwise will it be when Christians in Marseilles find themselves with an Algerian Muslim family next door; when a Dutch family in Rotterdam shares a neighbourhood with Muslims from Indonesia; when a German in the Ruhr works in the same factory as Muslims from Turkey; when a housewife in Bradford pushes her trolley round a supermarket behind a nervous, slow-moving, rather hesitant, Muslim woman from Pakistan; when your garage attendant in Birmingham is a Sikh; when a Hindu nurse ministers to your most intimate needs in hospital.

This is what neighbourhood means in practice. Conversation at this level will be far-removed from the Olympian heights where learned men of varying Faiths meet, somewhat removed from real life, and seek to understand each other across the abyss of language. About this we must think in a later chapter.

No, conversation at this domestic level will consist primarily in friendship, little courtesies, helpfulness, patience with strange customs and even stranger smells. It will call for much understanding of language difficulties, and will seek means to help with these. It will demand sensitivity to the fact that these neighbours of another Faith are a minority community, acutely nervous as to their security, and in no way anxious to be assimilated to our cultural environment. It is their own culture, with its religious overtones or undertones, which gives them psychic security. First they must see Jesus *in* us before we talk about Jesus. They can be with Jesus in our prayers from the start. But it may be a very long time before they 'touch the hem of his garment', still longer before they say 'Rabboni'. And they may never do either. Our responsibility is to be Jesus to them. This applies, incidentally, to *all* our neighbours.

In the next chapter we will look more closely at some of the very different ways in which Christians are trying to face the fact of religious pluralism and what it means for obedience to the Great Commission. Let this chapter end with some words of a Muslim scholar, Dr. L. O. Sanneh, who some years ago was led by his study of the references to Jesus in the Qur'an to become a Christian. He is the author of an important survey of Muslims in Britain. He ends his survey with these words—

Christians must be encouraged to accept and rejoice in a multi-faith Britain. Because the Church has for so long been portrayed as in the throes of a crisis people have become perplexed and this has left the hangover of a crisis mentality. But a pluralistic religious world is not a crisis. It is God's providential challenge and the Church's opportunity. It does not destroy anything except our complacency and smugness. It is the opening through which God's call for his people today has become searchingly but compassionately focussed.

CHAPTER 9

The Christian Response to Religious Pluralism

'GOD'S PROVIDENTIAL CHALLENGE and the Church's opportunity.' Can we look at the fact of religious pluralism like this? I believe we can and should. The Church of the Roman Empire faced it and was unafraid. The accident of Europe's isolation in the Middle Ages, and then its successful expansion in the following centuries, obscured the realities of religious pluralism from most Christians of the West. But missionaries, and those who responded to the gospel, knew it in their own experience. It is only in the recent past that the reality of religious pluralism has come to be recognised by western Christians as creating unexpected and unwelcome problems. This is what is new, not religious pluralism.

Now, if we are, indeed, to see in this new situation 'God's providential challenge and the Christian's opportunity', we must be ready for hard thinking, some of it very unfamiliar. We have, to begin with, to take with the utmost seriousness the spiritual experience reflected in other great religions of mankind. We have to go on to ask what this experience means for Christians. Other men are never just an object of Mission. Always, they say something to us. Can we believe that sometimes it is God who, through them, is speaking to us?

As we saw in the last chapter, the men of other Faiths are no longer 'over there', so that we can send missionaries to convert them. Now, they are 'over here', and are sending missionaries to convert us! This also is very new.

One further important fact about our present experience is

that we have also to take very seriously those quasi-religions which challenge the core of *every* Faith, including our own. Secular humanism, Communism, the crude worship of material prosperity, all equally deny any point of ultimate reference, to know Whom is life, not to know Whom is death. The necessary limitations of this book allow no possibility here to develop the challenge of these quasi-religions. But it will be a disastrous miscalculation if we ignore their importance.

In this chapter I will attempt to describe how various Christian thinkers are viewing the task of obedience to the great commission. In a short space it will be impossible to do justice to their thinking. What I offer may even be a caricature, though that is not my wish. In the bibliography at the end of the book will be found listed some of the most valuable of their writings in which they speak for themselves. For my part, I have one real embarrassment. One, at least, of those whose views I query and would wish to supplement, is a very dear friend who is on my daily prayer list. Another has been a most gracious and patient correspondent. Others have stretched my mind in ways that make me ever their debtor. In the pursuit of truth, courtesy and respect for the other man's opinions is a golden rule.

I list seven, more or less distinct approaches to our subject, and ask, 'are they adequate?'

(1) The Church as the sacrament of humanity
This is a view which is being found very attractive by a number of Roman Catholic writers. It has been expressed by one of them in the words — 'Christ present in the Church as the fundamental sacrament of God's love pours out that love into the whole world for its consecration. This is the mission'.

Another has put it like this—

It would seem reasonable...to interpret the mission of the Christian Church in terms of a representative function involving both service and redemptive suffering. Christians will indeed preach Christ universally. Their witness to Christ, when offered without arrogance, will have many indirect effects, apart from direct conversions. And these direct conversions themselves should be regarded, not as the first steps in gathering all men unto the Christian Church as a visible community on earth, but as God's election of some for a special representative role.

That is nobly stated. All the writers in this tradition are impressed with the sheer dimension of the Christian task in a world in which the population explosion means that the proportion of Christians to the whole is steadily diminishing. Furthermore, they take seriously the fact that the other great religions, far from being on the point of collapse, are experiencing something of a renaissance. From being on the defensive, they are moving to the attack, offering to the world a global alternative to Christianity.

For this view of the Church as a 'representative' community there is certainly good basis in Scripture in the doctrine of the 'Remnant'. Isaiah's prophecies are surely akin to this view, as would seem to be the general purpose of God for Israel, as it is unfolded in the Old Testament.

There is no question among these thinkers and writers but that the great commission stands. 'Wherever preaching is possible and meaningful,' writes one, 'it must be done. Its fulfilment lies in an extension of missionary work into spheres which are not charted by missionary statistics.' That is a useful reminder of the strictly limited value of all statistical assessments of the value of missionary work. Scripture provides no justification whatever for taking statistics seriously. This is one of the quantitative fallacies of far too much missionary thinking. Quality is undefinable and known only to God.

This point of view which is here briefly summarised has been argued with great cogency and with deep humility in three books which I would commend to the reader— *Christ and the World Religions* by Charles Davis; *Christian Revelation and World Religions,* a book of essays by various writers and edited by Joseph Neuner; and *Towards a Theology of Religions* by Heinz Robert Schlette.

A query as to the complete adequacy of the view is, I think, legitimate. For Roman Catholics, the monolithic structure of the post-Tridentine Church, with its exclusive claim to be the Church, did offer a pattern upon which the idea of the Church as a sacrament of humanity could be developed. But is this a serious possibility for the post-Vatican II Roman Church, which now eschews that dogmatic exclusivism? In what sense can the Christian Church, in its myriad divisions, be said to be either representative or sacramental? Individual Christians, in given circumstances, can be both. But in what sense is this true of the Church? A fully united Christian Church could discharge such a role. But what is the nature of the unity which the Roman Church, and the whole ecumenical movement, are seeking? It is tacitly assumed that it must be, in some sense, a unified institutional structure. But how can a unified structure do justice to the diversity of human nature? What is the theological significance of differences of understanding and of response to the grace of God? So far, little progress has been made to answering these fundamental questions.

Yet we may not dismiss the truth which is being set forth in this approach. Jesus, our Lord, as our representative is the enduring intercessor for the world (Heb. 7:25). We can strive to embody this intercession in corporate ways. A remnant can be redemptive as 'salt to the world', 'light for all the world' (Matt. 5:13-14). But this is not the same thing as saying that the Church, as an institution, is the sacrament of humanity.

(2) Salvation through conscience

This very widely shared conviction has been stated as follows— 'A real concrete chance of salvation exists for every individual, provided he lives according to his conscience, that is to say by ethical principles, and honestly and honourably in his individual circumstances'. A basis for this conviction is the certainty that other religions than Christianity enshrine many profound truths. Again, that among those who follow them are men and women of the utmost probity and real holiness of life cannot be denied by any who have had the privilege of knowing such. This position can be expressed in the form of three questions.—

1. We explain the fact that the Milky Way is there by the doctrine of creation, but how do we explain that the Bhagavad Gita is there?

2. We watch the deeply devout Muslim or Hindu at his prayers, and we ask, 'does God listen to them?' We answer, 'Yes' because we cannot limit the operation of the Spirit of God.

3. Is not Romans 2:11-16 decisive?

A corollary to the belief in the possibility of salvation through obedience to conscience was expressed in a conference on 'Christian Revelation and non-Christian Religions' held in Bombay in 1964. Cardinal Bea, of the Roman Church, felt able to say, with the authority of Vatican II behind him, that —

> those who live according to the command of their right conscience are united to Christ and his mystical body through implicit faith, pending the time when they recognise fully the riches of Christ and share in them. There can be no doubt that the Church in her dialogue with them effectively endeavours to lead them to an explicit and full participation in these riches.

'Implicit faith' is a technical term, and means that within the limits of your understanding you are a 'believer'. This doctrine is held to justify the reckoning of many as being, in fact, 'anonymous Christians'.

We agree that conscience, as a personal possession, is implanted in every man by God. We can take with complete trust Paul's words, 'God judges the secrets of human hearts through Christ Jesus. So my gospel declares' (Rom. 2:16). There are depths beyond depths to be plumbed in those words, 'through Christ Jesus'. But the simple meaning remains clear. It is a very important part of our Gospel to every man.

What, however, we must surely go on to say is, that Paul's argument did not end at Romans 2:16. Man's conscience is in greater or lesser degree sadly distorted, for 'all alike have sinned, and are deprived of the divine splendour' (Romans 3:23). When Paul goes on to add that 'all are justified by God's free grace alone, through his act of liberation in the person of

Christ Jesus…(vs 24 ff), he is arguing specifically about the negative value of the Torah as a means of salvation. We might paraphrase Paul's argument by saying, 'no religion is a means of salvation', and this applies to all religions, including Christianity. There are, then, no *ordinary* ways of salvation. There is only the *extraordinary* way which is Jesus Christ himself. It is response to him which saves, even when, as may often be the case, he is unrecognised as the Saviour. All religions, *qua* religions, stand under that judgment. We Christians do well to remember that judgment begins at the house of God (Jer. 26, and 1 Peter 4:17).

Romans, Chapter 7 gives one man's experience of the agonising limitations of conscience as a way of salvation, a common experience in all religions.

(3) Feeding the multitude

There is a widespread belief among many good Christian people that their obligation to fulfil the great commission has been adequately met by their giving generously to one or other of the agencies concerned with feeding the world's hungry people.

We have already seen how important a 'sign of the times' is the remarkable growth of human compassion. That he who had such compassion on the multitude rejoices in our care and concern for the needy cannot be doubted. Moreover, it is more than possible that the devoted labours of fund-raising agencies for meeting desperate human need are having a measurable effect in opening the eyes of politicians and business-men to their own long-term interests. The under-developed world is a combustible mixture which may soon explode.

The appeal of the hungry goes even further. There is a widespread sense that, in providing for the hungry, entirely without regard to their religious beliefs, but only for their hunger, there is the best way of relating ourselves to the people of other Faiths. The gibe about 'rice-Christians' cannot, historically speaking, be easily dismissed. To our shame, there is truth in it.

Let us be agreed then, that feeding the hungry is emphatically part of the Christian Mission— 'If a man has enough to live on, and yet when he sees his brother in need shuts up his heart against him, how can it be said that love for God dwells in him?' (1 John 3:17 margin). There can be no argument about this. Yet we can insist that this is a part, it cannot be the whole, of Mission.

We do not preach to a starving man. But, having met his immediate physical need, we may well find that he has an empty mind. His need now may well be to learn how he can feed himself. Much of the most valuable work of Christian Aid and other similar enterprises is directed to this end. Some of the most imaginative activities in which Christians are cooperating today lie in encouraging the development, in the poorer countries, of an Intermediate Technology, a way of harnessing modern science to local resources. This is well illustrated in E.F. Schumacher's important book, *Small is Beautiful,* an economic manual as full of good theology as it is of common sense.

With the belly full and the mind stimulated, and with hope re-born, the man of whom we are thinking is likely to begin asking himself some fundamental questions about himself, his neighbour, and even God. To these questions there are many answers. But there is a Christian answer, and the great commission is not obeyed when that answer is with-held.

(4) Mission as liberation

'By what apostolic authority may we conflate liberation from sin, death and the demonic, with liberation from injustice, oppression and poverty? In more personal terms, how do we relate the first-century activities of Jesus and Paul with the twentieth century activities of Ché Guevara and Camilo Torres? Are they similar, repetitious, distinguishable, or unre-lated?' These are not academic questions. They are flung out by José Miguez Bonino from the furnace of conflict which is raging through Latin America today. In his book, *Revolution-ary Theology comes of Age,* he most movingly surveys both the actual situation of desperate human need in his continent, and what a representative group of Christian thinkers are saying and doing about it.

In the previous section we saw the way in which the hunger of the Third World is moving the conscience of Western Christians. In Latin America this is being viewed at close quarters, not just as hunger of the body, but also as intolerable social injustice at every level of human life, injustice enthroned in the structures of social and political life, and heavily underwritten by the investing public of North America and Europe.

What do you do when every possible constitutional effort has been frustrated by the powers that be? When violence itself is the subtle, but all-pervasive social and political practice of the rulers, what alternative is left to the ruled but violence? In Latin America these are burning questions of life and death. What is the Christian to *do* in such circumstances, *do* and not just *think?* Archbishop Camara is wrestling with this question. Hundreds of Roman priests and Protestant pastors are active in their demand for radical political change. A few priests have actually become guerrilla fighters. How are we to judge these things?

Most of those who are writing on this subject, as Bonino makes clear, hesitate at the stark question— 'If I, as a Christian, get the enemy in my sights, do I pull the trigger?' But once involved in the struggle for justice, that may become a real question. It was real enough for Bonhoeffer and von Trott, and many others, in Germany. They found themselves, after a real agony of doubt, compelled to 'pull the trigger', and paid for their decision with their lives, their eyes wide open to the inevitability of paying just that price.

Christians in Latin America are clear only about this, that it is part of the very Mission of the Church to be identified with the struggle of the poor and deprived for justice. That is how they understand our Lord's choice of a text, as we have it in Luke, Chapter 4. What must surely be clear for us, the further away we are from the conflict, is to be certain that our answers are neither easy nor glib.

But some of these fellow-Christians of ours are also deeply aware that the substitution by force of the rule of the oppressed over the oppressors is all too likely to enthrone a new oppressor. There are plenty of object lessons of this truth elsewhere in the world. Let us try to feel the pain and the strain of Christian leadership in such circumstances.

Jacques Ellul has given us one of the most penetrating studies of violence. He is completely committed to the most vigorous protest at every possible level, in season and out of season. He believes that the Christian, confronted by injustice, must make his protest on behalf of the sufferer, whatever punishment he himself may have to suffer. But he is clear that physical force is not the answer. He writes of the 'spiritual violence' of love. He fortifies himself with Paul's word that evil is to be overcome with good (Rom. 12: 17-21), itself an echo of the insistence of Jesus in the 'Sermon on the Mount', and demonstrated by him on Calvary. This is no easy programme.

That Ellul is not playing with words is well illustrated by the heroic witness of Beyers Naudé in South Africa. Refusing to pass judgment on the victims of violence who have taken the way of violence, he is yet clear that 'this is not, and cannot be, and never will be the truly satisfying answer which God has made available to his children on earth'. He believes that there is a dimension of divine power and moral force which the Church has never been able to grasp and act upon. And then he adds —

One of the essential elements which would be required to operate in order to allow this moral force to display itself is that of voluntary individual and communal suffering on the part of those involved in the struggle for human dignity and justice. I believe that the Christian community throughout the world needs to reflect much more deeply on the nature of suffering, especially as it has been exemplified through the life and death of Christ, in order to give a more satisfying answer than the Christian Community has done up till the present day.

Here is a dimension of the great commission which is always in danger of being overlooked. In a world which is becoming daily more violent, even Christians, still comfortable in their suburban ghettoes, would be well-advised to begin some of that reflection commended by Beyers Naudé. There may not be much time left.

(5) The way of dialogue

Dialogue is to be understood, first and foremost, as the occasion of a meeting of persons. There is no such thing as a dialogue of religions, but only a dialogue between men of religion. Much unnecessary confusion would be saved if this vital distinction were always observed when talking about dialogue.

Now, if there is to be a real meeting, for instance, between myself and a man of another Faith, it is necessary, before even one word is spoken, that both shall share a certain attitude. For my part, I have to begin by accepting that the other man is, like myself, a man with a living faith which determines how he thinks and lives. He will accept me in the same way. That attitude comes first. But if there is to be a real meeting between two people, we both have to realise that each of us has behind him a particular history. These particular histories can be a serious barrier to any mutual understanding.

A missionary in North India, Roger Hooker, with a considerable experience of dialogue at the everyday level, and being himself a fluent linguist, has suggested that in order to go forward to mutual understanding, there is a prior necessity to take three steps backward. As he has written— 'The creation of a common language is a pre-condition for any genuine dialogue with men of other Faiths, and indeed with many of one's own Faith, for the problem exists within religions and not just on the frontiers between them.' Before the common language can be achieved, the first step backward, he would say is to recognise frankly that we are talking two different languages. This is no easy step, because it is a common enough experience to realise that the other person has not understood what I am saying. The second step is much more difficult: 'it is to translate what the other man has said from his language into mine', so that I understand him. The same step has to be taken by him.

Roger Hooker then asks for a third step, which is even more difficult. This involves the uncovering of certain tacit assumptions, those presuppositions which govern all our thinking, the other man's and mine. He and I speak from these assumptions, rather than about them. Each of us, because these assumptions are unconscious, thinks that what he says is self-evidently true. But it is far from that. Each has to learn the language of the other. Only then can our minds meet so that each knows where he is.

This missionary's experience, which I have paraphrased, has far-reaching implications and should cure anyone of the idea that genuine religious dialogue, as distinct from religious chatter, is easy of attainment.

Let us, for our purpose here, assume that we have taken three steps backward, and are now going forward together to understand each other. This understanding is much more than an intellectual exercise. It has something in it of the nature of love. I want to 'feel what he feels' about the truths by which he lives. He does the same. Now, as someone has asked, 'Can anyone ultimately "understand" unless he commits himself?' This means for me that I must expose myself humbly to this friend. All I ask from him is that he will expose himself to me. From this mutual experience a new relationship is created. Eventually, this is the creative achievement of dialogue.

Two points remain to be made. Both of us are 'men of faith'. But some would argue that for dialogue on religious matters to be genuine, each party has to suspend his own deepest convictions during the dialogue. There is a technical term for this suspension, *epoché*. I would suggest that this is, properly speaking, undesirable and, if we are both men of integrity, it is impossible. For, if he and I are to be honest with each other, we must bring to our talking the whole of ourselves. In doing so we shall become very vulnerable. Only so will there be a meeting at depth. *Epoché* is an illusion; more, it is an evasion not open to the man of any Faith.

There is a second point about which there is much misunderstanding. Let us be quite clear that dialogue, as here defined, is not evangelism. It is an exercise in friendship in its own right, and must be pursued as right in itself. What may happen when friendship at this level is achieved is, quite literally in the hands of God, and should be left in his hands. To make this distinction in no way undermines the Christian's concern to communicate the Gospel and *vice versa*. But the other man's vulnerability is not to be exploited. For the Christian, the 'courtesy of Christ' must be the pattern of his behaviour.

While on this subject, it is of some importance to be aware that there are many men of other Faiths who view the widespread Christian interest in 'dialogue' with great suspicion. They view it as being no more than a change of front. Instead of the way of controversy which characterised much Christian missionary activity in the past, this subtle approach is being explored. This is disconcerting. But those who think of dialogue as a form of evangelism justify this suspicion. Let us be more modest, and see that dialogue is a valuable way in which we can meet men of other Faiths and in which they can meet Christians. In a religiously plural world, meeting is important.

(6) The conversion of Religion

In 1913 a book was published with the title, *The Crown of Hinduism*. The author, J. N. Farquhar, was a missionary working in Bengal. The essence of his argument was that there were many true religious insights in Hinduism, which reflected a religious quest whose goal would be found in Christ. There was, already, in some missionary circles, the beginning of a new respect for the spiritual insights of other Faiths. Somewhat over-easily, what appeared implicit in the title of this book was widely welcomed, without due attention being paid to Farquhar's own qualification of his hopes.

There was a real truth in what Farquhar was saying, and the mood of which I have spoken, if at times superficial, was an attempt to redress the balance of a former contemptuous dismissal of other men's religious convictions.

In considering our obedience to the great commission, it is always important to distinguish between profound spiritual impulses, which are the moving of the Holy Spirit of God, and the local clothing in which such impulses dress themselves. There was no contempt in Paul's words at Athens when he said, 'What you worship but do not know — this is what I now proclaim' (Acts 17:23). Give that word, 'know', its full value, and much that is partial and incomplete will be found in our own Christian knowing. We Christians are for ever having to check our worship and reject our idols. In this respect, Christians and Hindus, Muslims and Buddhists, Jews, and everyone else, all stand under the Word. This is not to say that there are no differences which distinguish the religions, that all are equally valid ways to the summit. It is to say that we all stand under the judgment and mercy of God. There is no place for crude triumphalism at that judgment seat. Such a reckoning by the Christian enables him to see where and how the judgment and mercy of God are at work in the religious aspirations of other men, the while he himself checks his own. Those who would see this positive humility graciously and brilliantly worked out cannot do better than get hold of the writings of Bishop Kenneth Cragg, beginning with *The Call of the Minaret*. Farquhar was a pioneer.

In more contemporary form, there is the serious attempt being made by many to explore the depths that are to be found in the spirituality that is present in other Faiths. To take but two examples: Constance Padwick's book, *Muslim Devotions — A Study of Prayer Manuals in Common Use* is a revelation, as, in the setting of India, is Klaus Klostermaier's *Hindu and Christian in Vrindaban*.

In all this exploration there is no reductionist view of Jesus Christ, our Lord. Rather, a fresh discovery is being made of his glory, convinced as all these explorers are, that he is the heart of all spirituality. The humble role of the Christian is to unveil the unknown Christ. What the unveiled Christ will do, once truly seen, is not for us to prophesy. He could be rejected.

One of these explorers is Raymond Panikkar, who does go so far as to speak of the conversion of religions, though he uses the word, conversion in a particular sense. I quote:-

Christianity in India, to take one example, should not be an imported, fully-fledged and highly developed religion, but Hinduism itself *converted* — or Islam, or Buddhism whatever it may be. It has to be added immediately that this Hinduism is, substantially, the same as the old one and yet something different, a new creature. The process of conversion implies a death and resurrection, but just as the risen Christ, or the baptized person is the same as previously and yet is a new being, likewise converted Hinduism is the true risen Hinduism, the same and yet renewed, transformed.

Raymond Panikkar is a very beloved and revered friend, and I think I know what he is struggling to express in words, both here and in all his writings. His passionate devotion to Jesus is the dynamic of all his thinking. But I would take the liberty to doubt whether he is not using the word too loosely when he talks about the *conversion* of a religion. The enormous complex of custom and culture and history which is Hinduism, amorphous and yet corporate, cannot, as such, experience a *metanoia*. What we can most surely say, and ought to say, is that, when Christianity becomes genuinely Indian, is no longer felt as an import, but is experienced as an Indian response to Jesus Christ, *then* spiritual forces will be let loose in India whose possibilities are strictly incalculable. What this will do to Hinduism we cannot even guess. Meanwhile, let us plunge into India.

Wilfred Cantwell Smith, another of my teachers, has made this important point. He writes — 'One of the facile fallacies that students of comparative religion must early learn to outgrow is…the supposition that the differing religions give differing answers to the same questions. We would hold rather that their distinctiveness lies in considerable part in a tendency to ask different questions'.

To that I would add that the Christian believes that God has asked Man one supreme question, 'Jesus Christ, who is he?' That is a question which no religion can answer, but only religious men.

(7) The Copernican Revolution

The old Ptolemaic view of the universe saw the earth as the centre round which the sun, the planets, and the stars revolved. It was Copernicus who established the fact that, far from the earth being the centre of the universe, it was only a satellite in orbit round the sun.

It is a legitimate analogy to say that a similar Ptolemaic view of themselves is common to all the religions, and has certainly been the traditional view taken for granted by Christians. This view is being challenged today by our far greater knowledge of what the other World-Faiths mean to the best of their adherents, and by the sheer fact of propinquity, as adherents of these other Faiths become our neighbours. The inescapable fact of religious pluralism does, for many people, call in question the traditional Christian assumptions. This is notably the case with the young, who are not disposed to accept traditional views, anyhow: but not only with the young. Many today, bitterly disillusioned with the materialistic rat-race of the Western World, and the apparent lack of any moral purpose in the policies of the western nations, are turning, in particular, to the East in quest of a spiritual experience they seem unable to find in the West.

If the universe does possess any ultimate meaning; if spiritual experience is as valid in its own sphere as mathematics, then the different religions can be viewed as planets revolving round the object of man's ultimate concern. And you can call that Ultimate Concern 'God' if you like.

This is a very widespread view. What is more, it is an understanding of the spiritual world shared by Hindus and Buddhists, the very source to which so many are turning for enlightenment. Some of the most brilliant apologists for Hinduism, men like Vivekananda, Radhakrishnan and Mahatma Gandhi, to mention only a few, presented this conviction with passion and enthusiasm.

A Western theologian who has, in his writing, given a prominent place to just such thinking is Professor Hick of Birmingham. In his book, *God and the Universe of Faiths*, he makes very effective play with this same analogy of Ptolemaic as distinct from Copernican thinking, with particular reference to Christian theology.

We have already noted that there are profound spiritual truths in other Faiths, truths which we should gladly acknowledge, and from which we have much to learn. Indeed, unless we can believe in the authenticity of all spiritual truth, wherever found, there would be no basis from which to communicate the gospel. But we are entitled to point out a serious weakness in the analogy if pressed too far. The planets circle endlessly. They never reach anywhere, let alone each other. Religions do not converge any more than planets. What the comparative study of religions is confirming is that, confronted with the ultimate mysteries of life and death, the spiritual resources of men everywhere are, in a real sense, comparable. This is hardly surprising seeing that 'the living God who made heaven and earth and everything in them...has not left *us* without some clue to his nature' (Acts 14:15-17).

What, however, we are, indeed, seeing is a convergence of religious men. And they are converging on the Man, Jesus. Whereunto this will grow we cannot tell, but it is happening. Let three illustrations point the direction. Muslim poets in the Arabic-speaking world are, to the scandal of the orthodox, finding in the historical Crucifixion some explanation of their peoples' sufferings. Among Jews, not least in Israel, there is a new interest in the man, Jesus, himself a Jew. After all, that is the way in which Andrew and Peter, James and John first got to know him. In his recent book, *Man and the Universe of Faiths*, M. M. Thomas, a leading Christian thinker in India, insists that 'it is not...the mystic Christ but the historical Jesus who has made the deepest impact upon Hinduism'. And there is much complementary evidence of this convergence upon the Man. The Christ of the Andes is no longer a statue, but is taking flesh and blood in the tormented struggles of the peoples of Latin America. He comes striding out of Gulag Archipelagos. On the very morning when I was writing these words, an undergraduate/of an English university said on the radio, 'What the hippies are looking for is what Jesus called Love.' Whether it be from the lips of babes, or through the experience of the wrath of God, praises are converging on Jesus, the Jesus of history.

So, when Professor Hick presses his analogy and asks, 'Do we regard the Christian way as the only way, so that salvation is not to be found outside it; or do we regard the other great religions of mankind as other ways of life and salvation?', we reply that these are not the real questions raised either by contemporary knowledge or by contemporary events. 'Other ways of life' there certainly are, and in and through them men are seeking salvation. The real question is, 'What is the significance of the convergence of so many seekers on the Jesus of history?' I believe that the simple answer is that Jesus offers a quality of salvation which, slowly but surely, men are coming to realise can be found nowhere else.

I do not press the evidence that I have described. It is far too slender. I am content simply to point to it and ask what it means. Meanwhile, the grounds for Christians believing that Jesus saves, heals, liberates in the way no other saviour does are twofold.

The *first* is the historic reality of the Event which we know as the Life and Death and Resurrection of Jesus Christ. That he lived is indisputable, except by those who find the challenge of that quality of living altogether too uncomfortable. That he died, is equally indisputable. That *something* happened three days later is again indisputable. Equally indisputable is the impact of that *something* on subsequent history. That millions today know this Jesus as their own contemporary is again indisputable — a real fact, be it noted, which is the direct result of the obedience of countless Christians of every race to the Great Commission himself and his commission to them.

Our *second* ground of belief in Jesus as the supreme revelation of the mind and purpose of God is, in its very essence, a conviction about the nature of the universe. It cannot be proved, but it can be lived. In the first chapter of John, in its opening verses, we see as in a mystery the oneness of the uncreated light, enlightening every man coming into the world, and then coming himself into the world as Man. That is to go back in time. In Colossians 1:13-20 and in Ephesians 1:10 and elsewhere, we see him at the end of time — the Omega figure, as he was and is the Alpha figure. This, as I must insist, is an act of faith. Christian experience suggests that it makes more sense as an interpretation of the past, present and future, than any other interpretation. Its corollary is, of course, the tremendous claim we Christians make for Christ. The more I claim for Jesus Christ and the inspiring activity of his Holy Spirit in creating and redeeming and sanctifying human life, the more profound is my reverence and regard for what I see him doing in history *and* in the lives of those who do not know him. 'Expect great things from God,' said William Carey, one of the great pioneers of the modern missionary movement: then we will 'attempt great things for God.' The trouble with far too many of us Christians is that our Christ, like our God, is far too small.

How exciting it is to live in a world of religious pluralism such as we are experiencing today. What a wonderful opportunity that religious pluralism offers to Christians and to everyone else to make a new discovery of Jesus Christ. How gratefully we should accept God's providential challenge.

CHAPTER 10

Obeying the Great Commission
Now and Tomorrow

THE GOSPEL IS for the *whole* man: for the *whole* of mankind:
and it is addressed to the *whole* natural order. But within
history, its progress towards its goal has had to be spelled out
in varying ways, in different contexts.

In the early centuries it proceeded by *infiltrating* a dominant
culture. Only a very few of its agents were wise, fewer still
were noble. They were, indeed, the 'offscourings' of the world.
But, in due course, they turned that world upside down.

During the next thousand years the shape of their task was
different. They had to bring *order out of chaos*. In so doing,
they created a civilisation.

Then came more than four centuries of *exploration*. This
was a geographical feat, but it was much more. The explorers
had also to discover the true relation of man to the natural
order, and, as well, to trace the contours of man himself. In the
process there were opened up for the first time, the possibilities
of unity for mankind. Glimpses, even, could be caught of that
'far-off divine event, to which the whole creation moves', the
wider harmony of the whole universe. The last is no fancy for
those who take Ephesians 1:10 and Colossians 1:20 seriously.

If those very rough generalisations may serve as showing the
underlying task of Christians, individually and corporately, in
the past, then perhaps the word, *incarnation* may be allowed to
denote the peculiar task of today and tomorrow.

The Gospel has now to be seen to 'become flesh', so that the
first 'Becoming' is made contemporary. This task is threefold.
First, this new becoming has to be seen as genuinely local in
expression everywhere. Then no less, it has to be seen as

having everywhere a family likeness, an influence making for unity. These are the congenial aspects of its task.

Much less congenial, in a world more hostile than for many centuries, it has to show that eternity is uncomfortably immediate. Man's treatment of man, and man's treatment of nature, are leading inexorably to disaster. Far from God being dead, it is man who will soon be dead if he does not start to take God seriously. The good news of the wrath of God has to be spelled out as the complement of the good news of his love. Such a spelling out once led to the Crucifixion. There is no reason to think that it may not lead the obedient to the same experience, followed as it surely will be by a similar resurrection.

Obeying the Great Commission today and tomorrow will be no easier than in the past. Matthew 24, Mark 13, Luke 21, John 16: 31-33, and the whole drama of the Passion Story, and the Book of the Revelation are part of the New Testament. They were not written in order to be explained away.

Meanwhile, our present task, the task of all who would be obedient, takes its pattern now as ever from the Great Commission himself. We have our calling made very clear in the first verse of Hebrews 3: 'Therefore, brothers in the family of God, who share a heavenly calling, think of the Apostle and High Priest of the religion we profess, who was faithful to God who appointed him'. The apostleship of Jesus himself finds frequent echo in the record of John. Two passages are particularly important for us. 'This is the work that God requires: believe in the one whom he has sent. (John 6:29); and 'As the Father sent me, so I send you' (John 20:21). The word translated 'sent' is the verbal form of the word, Apostle. The witness of the other Gospels shows that this was the underlying conviction of all the teaching of Jesus. He was the Apostle of God, sent into the world with a message from God, which message he was.

This word, 'apostle', together with its verbal forms, runs like a gold thread through the New Testament. But, in practice, as a word, it is virtually confined *today* to a strictly limited ecclesiastical use. Its true English equivalent, the *only* one, is the word, 'missionary', that is, 'one sent on a Mission with a message'. The word is now familiar in secular as well as religious contexts. This is a very great advantage, for it helps to disinfect this very great word from some of its less happy associations in the nineteenth century. In all that follows I will be using the word, 'missionary' with the scriptural significance of 'apostle' in mind, and always in ultimate relation to the Apostle and High Priest of our profession.

Because misunderstanding is sometimes almost woefully easy, we should be clear that the word, 'missionary' is to be understood as applying to anyone, anywhere, who is committed to obedience to the great commission. That obedience may, for most, be confined to their 'Jerusalem'. For some it may mean moving into neighbouring 'Judaea'. Others, perhaps, will find themselves unexpectedly in some uncongenial 'Samaria'. Still others will go to 'the ends of the earth'. All should be knit together in prayer, for their work is one. It should also be clear that the words, 'missionary' and 'Mission' are not to be restricted to individuals. They are equally relevant to group obedience. Ideally, they should refer to every congregation and to the universal Church.

So far, I have written as a Christian of the West. From now on, all I write, I write as a Christian who may be a Japanese or an Arab, a Korean or an Indian, a Persian or a Filippino, a Chinese or an African, or as one of any race or nation to whom a Christian may belong. Let us then consider the word, 'missionary' and the life and work of such a one, or such a company under seven aspects.

(1) The missionary as inquirer

If this aspect is put first, it is not because it is the most important, but because, in the sense in which it is used here, it is commonly neglected. Being an asker of questions means being curious about everything that affects the people whom the missionary is hoping to meet. These people live in a very practical world, in which their living is profoundly influenced by political, economic and social factors, of which even they themselves are not always aware. It is by being inquisitive about these matters that the missionary becomes their contemporary; and that is part of the meaning of 'incarnation'.

'Becoming flesh', in this fashion, implies being knowledgeable. It implies asking questions of people, but also of books and newspapers and the mass media. If we do not ask the questions we will get no answers at all.

A great commentator on the prophecy of Isaiah, George Adam Smith, is describing the political situation which lay behind Chapter 10: 5-34. For Isaiah and his contemporaries it looked as if the Assyrians were certain to invade and capture and destroy Jerusalem. An *atheism of fear* was obsessing the people.

> Isaiah's problem was thus the fundamental one between faith and atheism; but we must notice that it did not arise theoretically, nor did he meet it by an abstract proposition. This fundamental religious question —whether men are to trust in the visible forces of the world or in the invisible God — came up as a bit of practical politics. It was not to Isaiah a philosophical or theological question. It was an affair in the foreign policy of Judah.

The crucial point is that Isaiah saw foreign politics as involving moral judgments. This insight applies to all politics, national and local, as well as international. This illustration is susceptible of infinite adaptations. The missionary, in any situation, needs to be politically and socially sensitive to moral issues, and to help others to be the same.

This does not mean that he becomes an amateur politician. The missionary today, who serves in a country not his own, is very much a guest of the country as well as of the Church. He will quite certainly be viewed by some with a measure of suspicion as being politically unreliable. He will be watched. He owes it both to the country and the Church to be above suspicion as a meddler. That is why, the more alert he is to things as they are, the less likely he is to be taken by surprise by events. He will be immune to the atheism of fear, and will help to immunise others.

(2) The missionary as learner

The word, 'disciple' means a learner, and the missionary remains a learner to the end. We have seen him asking questions. Now he has to learn what are the real questions which the people he meets are asking. The more he discovers of these questions, the less ready he will be to imagine that he knows all the answers.

To discover what are the real questions people are asking means learning their language. The language may be that of a strange people: or the language of a strange younger generation of his own race: often, it will be the language of those of his own generation trained to think in ways foreign to his own experience.

Learning a language so that you really understand it, think in it, even dream in it, is a physically, mentally, and spiritually exhausting experience. But if we are to transpose the message with which we believe we have been entrusted in a way which will be understood, there is no escape from learning how the other man is thinking. And that involves learning how he is 'feeling', and his 'feelings' are the fruit of his own cultural inheritance. The missionary has much to learn, particularly so if he crosses a cultural frontier.

Klaus Klostermaier, in his book already referred to, comments on this last point. He tells how Hindu friends complained repeatedly that the Hindi of our Bible translation was no 'Hindi', but a 'foreign language'. The translators knew the grammar and dictionary, but not Hinduism. The logic of Klostermaier's plea was not less Hindi, but more. Unless and until we know a lot more about how Hindus use their own language, we shall never be able to use it ourselves so as to speak effectively and meaningfully about Jesus. That is authentic missionary experience.

There is some shrewd wisdom in a letter by a fourth-century writer, Evagrius, explaining to a friend about his translation of the life of St. Antony, which he has produced. He has had to translate from Greek into Latin, and he says—

> Direct word for word translation from one language into another darkens the sense and strangles it, even as spreading couchgrass a field of corn... For my part, to avoid this, I have so transposed this life of the Blessed Antony which you desired that whatever lack there may be in the words, there is none in the meaning. Let the rest go bat-fowling for letters and syllables: do you seek for the sense.

That is admirable advice for all missionaries, and particularly so for interpreters of the Bible.

Side by side with this care for learning the language, we need to be ever learning the implications of our common humanity. One contemporary phenomenon is the widespread emergence, especially among the young, of a growing consciousness of this underlying reality. Easily, it may lead to very superficial conclusions about all religious experience being equally valid, but it remains a very important phenomenon of our time. The 'hippie trail to the East' deserves understanding, for we, as Christians, believe that God's own image has been defaced, not destroyed, and that his purpose of a common salvation remains unchanged. That is our Christian conviction and the basis of our hope. Our realism can provide the corrective to superficial optimism by affirming the reality of our common sinfulness. As one missionary whom I know has put it— 'This means that the dividing line between good and evil does not pass between the Christian on the one hand and the Hindu, Buddhist or Muslim on the other — which is what we have all too readily assumed in the past — but between all of us men and the searching *judgment* of the divine word.' To learn that, for the missionary, will mean being very humble.

(3) The missionary as listener

There is a listening which obviously belongs to learning a foreign language. Without a musical ear, without some facility in catching the nuances in a tonal language, it is almost impossible to learn some languages. But the listening with which I am concerned here is 'listening' to people. This may involve crossing the ocean, or just crossing the road.

Listening to another person is a great deal more of an art than most of us realise. The true listener is giving all his attention to what the other person is saying, listening even to his silences.

A subtler point still is, that as I so listen, I become aware of myself listening. This is important for, unless I listen to myself listening I will be likely to assume, quite wrongly, that a word used in the context of my own experience means the same as in the experience of the one to whom I am listening. There is much wisdom as well as a proper courtesy in this sensitivity of listening.

Furthermore, if we are listening 'in the name of Jesus Christ', we have to listen to him as a partner in the conversation. This is not playing with words. For once we realise that he is listening, we must be ready to hear him speaking. He may say something we have never heard before. Given our concentrated attention, we may hear him speaking through the lips of the other person, be he an agnostic, a humanist, a Marxist, a Hindu, a Muslim, a Buddhist or a Jew — or anyone. This kind of listening can be very exciting. It is something every missionary must practise. Jesus, now as always, is very full of surprises.

(4) The missionary as lover

Several times in this book we have had occasion to speak of the patience of God. Would we be so very wrong were we to say that patience is the greatest of all his attributes? For what is patience but love in action; love waiting; love suffering; love pursuing; love ever respecting our freedom, however much we abuse it? If this is the supreme attribute of God, it must be the supreme attribute of the missionary. He, if he knows himself, knows that he has already tried the patience of God to the limit. He must show to others what God has shown to him.

Applicable to all missionaries in every situation, across the world or across the street, are some words spoken by Bishop Stephen Neill to a missionary group many years ago when he was still a missionary in India. He knew well how often those to whom he was speaking, out of sheer love for some individual, tried to force the pace of his flowering into Christian faith. Speaking to himself and to the group, he said—

Let us not mix up our affair and God's. It is our business to see that if possible the enquirer's face is turned to the light, and if possible that he is kept on the move. If he has left Ur of the Chaldees, that is a great thing. But it takes time to get all the way across the desert to the promised land; and it is our part to lose neither faith nor patience, but to emulate the patience of God.

That is a great parable. I quote another, this time from one of the nineteenth century pioneers in Iran, Dr Bruce. Writing home, he described his work as follows— 'I am not reaping the harvest; I scarcely claim to be sowing the seed; I am hardly ploughing the soil; but *I am gathering out the stones.* That too is missionary work, let it be supported by loving sympathy and fervent prayer.'

There is no accident in that both parables suggest something of a desert. The missionary, now and always, is faced with a desert in which his calling is to 'prepare a road for the Lord through the wilderness, clear a highway across the desert for our God' (Isa. 40:3).

If I take these illustrations from Asia, that is by the way. The parables are equally relevant to the desert of the English Midlands, to Chicago, to the Ruhr or Amsterdam, to Sao Paulo, Lagos or Nairobi. Loving will take many forms, each of them, in a real sense, a sacrament. The minister of the sacrament may be a shop-steward on the floor of a factory; a management consultant; a doctor or a nurse in a hospital; a teacher opening windows in the minds of pupils; a translator pursuing an elusive word to give sense to what he is translating; the hostess whose home is ever open to any visitor; the man or woman struggling across the desert of learning a foreign language; that through them the Word made flesh may win his way and 'pass the low lintel of the human heart'.

Being a missionary, anywhere, is to be a lover. There is no other way.

(5) The missionary as a link

The Christian Church exists all over the world. Its proportion, in relation to the total population, may be minute. In more places than one it is, for all practical purposes, proscribed. But it is there. In some places it is growing very fast indeed, though statistics are an unreliable yardstick of spiritual progress.

Now, the missionary, whose particular vocation it is to cross national or cultural frontiers, has a distinctive role besides any others which are here being considered. He, in a very special sense, is a sacrament of the universal Church. His presence is a visible assurance to the local Christian community that they are members of a world-wide fellowship. He can assure them that other Christians are remembering them in their prayers. Persevering in intercession is very difficult without some personal link with those for whom one intercedes. Further to this, the missionary has a unique role in interpreting that local community to their prayer-partners in the land from which he or she comes. This is a very responsible role indeed.

It must be looked for and hoped for and worked for, that the countries of the West from which, in the past, most missionaries to Asia and Africa and Latin America have come, will themselves be receiving missionaries from these other lands. They may not be 'wanted', they may even be resented, but they are certainly needed! Already, we know well the great value of visitors coming to Britain, for instance, from Asia and Africa, bringing with them the inspiration and challenge of their own discovery of Christ. But the visits are all too short. The day of the long-term missionary is, we hope, soon to dawn here.

'Long-term' is also still a relevant category for some missionaries from the West. All talk about a 'moratorium' on these foreign missionaries greatly over-simplifies a complex question. Commonly, such talk generalises from local situations where particular problems exist, and is rarely endorsed *without many qualifications* by the responsible leaders of the Churches of Africa and Asia.

An African from Kenya, with some slight exaggeration, recently put it thus — 'World tourists cannnot help the Church'. To make clear what he meant, he went on to say— 'Those who come must be people of God, ready to go along with others, to get submerged and to make mistakes; not tamed things, but those ready to initiate — partners in fact'. The English may be sketchy, but the sense is clear!

That Kenyan commentary deserves careful study. Tourists do not get 'submerged'. Their mistakes are crudities which, at most, cause passing offence. They are not the mistakes from which lessons can be learnt. A tourist cannot be a 'partner' in the creative sense for which that African is asking.

A 'moratorium' on financial aid from abroad is another question altogether. It is, as with 'foreign missionaries', a proper subject for negotiation as between partners. It is no fit subject for facile generalisations.

Another factor which has to be kept in mind is the continuing danger for a local Church of its becoming introverted, and thus isolated from the broad stream of the Christian Faith, and coming to hold that Faith, not in 'due proportion' but in varying degrees of imbalance.

Besides this, it helps to demonstrate the catholicity of the national Church to have other nationals working alongside.

Again, an English Christian who resents an Asian immigrant being appointed as churchwarden in his parish church is as spiritually irresponsible as an Asian Christian who objects to a foreign missionary holding any office in the local Church. One of them may be a racialist, the other a nationalist; both, in their reactions, are sub-Christian.

(6) The missionary as disturber

The parable of the leaven (Matt. 13:33) was concerned to make one special point which is frequently missed. The peculiar property of leaven is that it causes fermentation. What our Lord is saying is that the Kingdom of Heaven, by its very existence as a Society, sets up a ferment, excites attention, which may be very disturbing indeed.

Consider a typical illustration, to which innumerable parallels can be found. A Christian from the Southern Sudan goes to Omdurman in the overwhelmingly Muslim Northern Sudan. He and his fellow-Christians from the South have proved to be a considerable surprise. Some Muslims have been so impressed by the lives of the despised Christians from the South that they find their way to Christian worship, causing thereby no small ferment, from which much may grow. That is our Lord's parable in action.

Wordsworth's joy, his 'sense sublime of something far more deeply interfused' began with 'a presence that disturbs'. Any missionary presence is meant to be disturbing. Liberating men's spirits from the bondage of sin: their minds from the bondage of ignorance; their bodies from the bondage of hunger and disease: this may set up a mighty ferment indeed.

(7) The missionary as a 'sign of the end'

'The Christian hope is a frontier subject and uses a frontier language'. In saying this, the late Bishop Fison gives us a clue to many passages in the Bible which are very puzzling if they are taken literally. He also offers us another clue in an illuminating phrase, 'lovers' time', which is how he interprets some of the sayings of Jesus about 'eternal life' — that it is a timeless experience as, for example, 'This is eternal life: to know thee who alone art truly God, and Jesus Christ whom thou hast sent' (John 17:3).

It is in some such way that we are to understand the words of Jesus as reported by Matthew (24:14)— 'This gospel of the kingdom will be proclaimed throughout the earth as a testimony to all nations; and then the end will come.' This does not refer to some heavenly calendar for us to guess about. If ever words spoke of 'lovers' time', these do. And it is in this sense that the missionary is a 'Sign of the End'.

How strange it is that so many fail to challenge the wisdom, let alone the morality of exporting the instruments of physical death, while the export of a joy which conquers both death and sin is deplored as 'forcing religion on people'!

The missionary, by virtue of that impulse of urgency to which he is a witness, invites men to feel the power of God's love; to face the necessity of choice, whether to respond to or reject it; to accept the burden of responsibility for others; to confront the reality of death.

All this he does today as though the work in which he is engaged will last a thousand years. He will bring every talent that he possesses to the task in hand as a skilled 'master-builder...' (1 Cor. 3:10 ff.). He is present for tomorrow. He plays his part in a society for whose redemption he prays and works and offers himself. He is consciously part of the ongoing process of history. He is, as any other good citizen, a builder of a better order. He is *in* this world, as our Lord prayed that he would be (John 17:15). At the same time, he knows *both* that human sin and selfishness can frustrate God's purpose, bringing all to ruin and destruction, *and* that he may have misjudged God's timing. More even than that, he knows that this day may be his last. He is a frontiersman who knows that the coming of God's Kingdom in its fulness, whatever its form in this world and the next, is in the hands of God. In both respects he is a man overflowing with hope, serving as he does the God of hope, who is 'the source of all fortitude and all encouragement' (Rom. 15: 5,13). All this is only another way of affirming the fundamental emphasis of the New Testament that Jesus Christ is both present and coming.

In all these respects the missionary stands on the crucial frontiers of life. Through him the Holy Spirit 'confutes the world and shows where wrong and right and judgment lie' (John 16:8). To be a missionary anywhere is to accept a formidable vocation.

Under all these seven aspects we are to view the missionary calling. No one of these characteristics is new. They have always been the proper equipment of the missionary. But they need to be minted afresh. They need to be seen to be what they are, the indispensable qualifications for Mission in the very difficult and, in some ways, novel circumstances of our time.

In so defining the word 'missionary' and describing his mission, whether in terms of the individual, the group, or the Church as a whole, no attempt is made here to argue for this form of missionary activity or that. We cannot foresee the future. What we do see is an extremely perplexing world. Ancient stabilities have disappeared. We cannot affirm with any certainty that the patterns of institutional Church life, as traditionally understood, will survive. They may do so. On the other hand, they have disappeared in China, and not only there. Long ago they disappeared in North Africa, and have not reappeared. Behind the Iron Curtain the Church lives in perpetual tension with the several governments. Economic factors alone could radically change the shape of the Church in the rest of the world. Again, the pattern of Mission-crossing-frontiers may have to take forms in sharp contrast to what was commonplace, even twenty-five years ago. Indeed, this is already happening as, increasingly, institutional activities are being taken over by governments, activities which were once the normal pattern of work. We can face all this without either alarm or despondency. All the seven aspects of the missionary which we have considered will continue to be relevant for Mission until that day when the Great Commission himself will have seen the whole travail of his soul and is satisfied (Isaiah 53).

In common with all the books in this series, this one is, in some measure, a personal testimony as well as a personal interpretation. I would end it on a note of joy and hope and complete confidence. In doing so, I choose to quote a passage from a sermon preached by Dr. Martin Niemöller on the fourth Sunday in Lent, 1933, a difficult hour for those Christians in Germany who were seeking to be obedient to the Great Commission—

We have nothing to produce, nothing with which to appease the hunger of the multitude!...so that it may be visible to all eyes that we Christians are nothing ourselves; that we Christians have nothing ourselves; that we Christians do nothing ourselves! We live by a miracle, and this miracle is called Christ: he is everything; he has everything; he does everything.

That is the testimony which we as Christians owe to those who today come to us with their hopes and problems and expectations. We are not concerned with the question of how these crowds of unsettled men and women stand with regard to Christianity and the Christian Church; our duty is to see that these men and women meet the miracle called Christ!

I believe that the converted can face a great danger. It is that when the skill of Christ has brought us to him we forget about his children in concentration upon himself. It seems impossible, but we can almost forget the very suffering the thought of which was at one time driving us nearly mad. But Christ won't be concentrated upon in this one-sided manner. He won't have us on these terms. He is completely identified with all suffering creatures and we have him with them, or not at all. It can come about that some man or woman finds God not by way of a sense of unity with his children but through a journey as lonely as that of the Prodigal Son, but I believe that if we go home like the Prodigal Son we must go out again as the Good Samaritan.

Elizabeth Goudge
The Joy of the Snow — An Autobiography

This strictly limited book-list has been arranged roughly in relation to the three-fold division of the book. I hope the titles will indicate something of the range of available material. I have made no attempt to evaluate them. From my argument it will be obvious that, in a number of cases, I dissent from the conclusions of this author or that. Yet, from all these books I have learnt much. All are relevant to any serious attempt to understand the Christian Mission, as an historical phenomenon, and as a continuing commitment.

PART I

The Bible — Old and New Testaments

G. Bornkamm, *Jesus of Nazareth* (Hodder and Stoughton)

G. Dix, *Jew and Greek — A Study in the Primitive Church* (Dacre Press)

F. W. Dillistone, *The Significance of the Cross* (Westminster Press, Philadelphia)

C. H. Dodd, *The Founder of Christianity* (Collins)

Michael Green, *I believe in the Holy Spirit* (Hodder and Stoughton)

C. F. D. Moule, *The Phenomenon of the New Testament* (S.C.M.)

Stephen Neill, *Who is Jesus Christ?* (Lutterworth Press)

G. E. Ladd, *I believe in the Resurrection of Jesus* (Hodder and Stoughton)

Leon Morris, *I believe in Revelation* (Hodder and Stoughton)

W. M. Ramsay, *Pictures of the Apostolic Church* (Hodder and Stoughton)

W. M. Ramsay, *Pauline and other Studies* (Hodder and Stoughton)

Douglas Webster, *In Debt to Christ* (Highway Press)

PART II

R. Pierce Beaver, *To Advance the Gospel — selections from the writings of Rufus Anderson* (Eerdmans)

Peter Brown, *Augustine of Hippo — A Biography* (Faber & Faber)

Henry Chadwick, *The Early Church* (Pelican)

G. R. Cragg, *The Church and the Age of Reason* (Pelican)

John Foster, *After the Apostles* (S.C.M.)

John Foster, *The Church of the T'ang Dynasty,* (S.P.C.K.)

Michael Green, *Evangelism in the early Church* (Hodder and Stoughton)

S. L. Greenslade, *Shepherding the Flock* (S.C.M.)

S. L. Greenslade, *The Church and the Social Order* (S.C.M.)

Leslie Hardinge, *The Celtic Church in Britain* (S.P.C.K.)

Martin Jarrett-Kerr, *Patterns of Christian Acceptance* (O.U.P.)

R. Kilgour, *The Gospel in many parts* (B.F.B.S.)

Noel Q. King, *The Emperor Theodosius and the Establishment of Christianity* (S.C.M.)

David Knowles, *Saints and Scholars — Twenty-five Medieval Portraits* (C.U.P.)

E. Arno Lehmann, *It began at Tranquebar* (C.L.S. India)

A. J. Lewis, *Zinzendorf — the Ecumenical Pioneer* (S.C.M.)

J. B. Lightfoot, *The Apostolic Fathers* (Macmillan)

Philip Mason, *Prospero's Magic — some thoughts on Class and Race* (O.U.P.)

Stephen Neill, *A History of Christian Missions* (Pelican)

Stephen Neill, *The Christian Society* (Nisbet)

H. F. M. Prescott, *Jerusalem Journey — Pilgrimage to the Holy Land in the Fifteenth 'Century* (Eyre and Spottiswoode)

Ruth Rouse and Stephen Neill, *A History of the Ecumenical Movement — 1517-1948* (S.P.C.K.)

Paul Sabatier, *Life of St. Francis of Assisi* (Hodder and Stoughton)

Beryl Smalley, *The Study of the Bible in the Middle Ages* (Oxford, Clarendon Press)

R. W. Southern, *Western Society and the Church in the Middle Ages* (Pelican)

Jonathan Sumption, *Pilgrimage — An Image of Medieval Religion* (Faber and Faber)

J. Van den Berg, *Constrained by Jesus' Love* (J. H. Kok)

Laurens Van der Post, *The Dark Eye in Africa* (Hogarth Press)

Alec R. Vidler, *The Church in an Age of Revolution* (Pelican)

R. Voillaume, *Seeds of the Desert — The Legacy of Charles de Foucauld* (Burns and Oates)

Helen Waddell, *The Desert Fathers* (Constable)

Herbert B. Workman, *The Evolution of the Monastic Ideal* (Epworth Press)

PART III

J.N.D. Anderson, *Christianity and Comparative Religion* (Tyndale Press)

Peter Beyerhaus and Carl F. Hallencreutz (Ed.), *The Church crossing frontiers* (Gleerup, Uppsala)

José Miguez Bonino, *Revolutionary Theology comes of Age* (S.P.C.K.)

David Brown, *A Guide to Religions* (S.P.C.K.)

Kenneth Cragg, *The Call of the Minaret* (O.U.P.)

Kenneth Cragg, *Christianity in World Perspective* (Lutterworth Press)

Charles Davis, *Christ and the World Religions* (Hodder and Stoughton)

Jacques Ellul, *Violence* (S.C.M.)

J. E. Fison, *The Christian Hope — The Presence and the Parousia* (Longmans)

Norman Goodall, *Ecumenical Progress — A Decade of Change in the Ecumenical Movement, 1961-1971* (O.U.P.)

Carl F. Hallencreutz, *New Approaches to Men of Other Faiths* (World Council of Churches)

John Hick, *God and the Universe of Faiths — Essays in the Philosophy of Religion* (Macmillan)

W. A. Visser 't Hooft, *No Other Name* (S.C.M.)

W. A. Visser 't Hooft, ,*Memoirs* (S.C.M.)

Roger Hooker, *Uncharted Journey* (C.M.S.)

Alistair Kee (Ed.), *A Reader in Political Theology* (S.C.M.) (This is a valuable symposium of twenty-four writers)

Klaus Klostermaier, *Hindu and Christian in Vrindaban* (S.C.M.)

John A. Mackay, *Ecumenics — The Science of the Church Universal* (Prentice Hall, U.S.A.)

Donald McGavran, *Bridges of God* (World Dominion Press)

Donald McGavran, *Understanding Church Growth* (Eerdman's)

Jürgen Moltmann, *The Crucified God* (S.C.M.)

Stephen Neill, *The Christian Faith and Other Faiths* (O.U.P.)

Stephen Neill, *The Church and Christian Union* (O.U.P.)

J. Robert Nelson (Ed.), *No man is alien — Essays on the unity of mankind* (E.J. Brill, Leiden)

Joseph Neuner (Ed.), *Christian Revelation and World Religions* (Burns and Oates)

Martin Niemöller, *First Commandment* (William Hodge)

J. Edwin Orr, *The Eager Feet — Evangelical Awakenings, 1790-1830.* (Moody Press, Chicago)

J. Edwin Orr, *The Flaming Tongue — The Impact of 20th Century Revivals* (Moody Press, Chicago)

J. Edwin Orr, *The Fervent Prayer — The World-wide impact of the Great Awakening of 1858* (Moody Press, Chicago)

Constance E. Padwick, *Muslim Devotions — A Study of Prayer-Manuals in Common Use* (S.P.C.K.)

Raymond Panikkar, *The Unknown Christ of Hinduism* (Darton, Longman & Todd)

S. J. Samartha (Ed.), *Living Faiths and the ecumenical movement* (World Council of Churches)

S. J. Samartha (Ed.), *Dialogue between men of living faiths* (World Council of Churches)

Heinz Robert Schlette, *Towards a Theology of Religions* (Burns and Oates)

E. F. Schumacher, *Small is Beautiful* (Abacus)

Wilfred Cantwell Smith, *The Faith of other men* (The New American Library of World Literature)

Wilfred Cantwell Smith, *Questions of Religious Truth* (Victor Gollancz)

John Stott, *Christian mission in the modern world* (Falcon Books)

Bengt Sundkler, *(Church of South India — The Movement towards Union, 1900-1947* (Lutterworth Press)

John V. Taylor, *The Primal Vision* (S.C.M.)

John V. Taylor, *The Go-Between God* (S.C.M.)

William Temple *Basic Convictions* (Hamish Hamilton)

M.M. Thomas, *Man and the Universe of Faiths* (C.L.S. India)

Paul Tillich, *Christianity and the Encounter of the World Religions* (Columbia University Press)

C. Peter Wagner, *Frontiers in Missionary Strategy* (Moody Press, Chicago)